To love language is to love all mankind.

DICTIONARY OF
SAKSEN

A CONSTRUCTED PAN-GERMANIC LANGUAGE

JOHN C. RICKER

TRILLIUM PRESS

Dictionary of Saksen
a constructed Pan-Germanic language
by John C. Ricker

Compiled by Kat Ricker
Foreword by Kat Ricker with contributions by Paul Bierly

Design & production by Tom Sumner
Cover art by Angelina Marino-Heidel

Published on 30 September, 2019

©2019 Trillium Press
Portland, Oregon
ISBN 978-0-578-59661-7

CONTENTS

FOREWORD

by Kat Ricker, with contributions by Paul Bierly

A MAN WHO lives an interesting and productive life can distinguish himself in many different ways. John Charles Ricker certainly did that. Born in the tiny town of Nanty Glo, Pennsylvania, he grew up in a large first-generation Finnish family, who picked out their Americanized surname from a phonebook (going from Gnuttila to Ricker because "it could sound English or German"). He graduated with the Class of 1955 from Burton High School in Ohio. He enlisted in the Air Force, and got on a train that took him to Montana to begin four years of service to his country (Airman 2nd Class) and his college education, at University of Montana.

John graduated in 1962 from Ohio University with a Bachelor's Degree of Science in Education, and then received his Master's Degree in English from Bowling Green University in 1970, graduating Valedictorian of his Class.

He became a locally distinguished educator. John taught English in Northeast Ohio, first at Chardon High School 1962-1963, and then Jefferson High School from 1963 until his retirement in 1996. After retiring, he remained active and connected to his community.

John also worked as a bartender on Saturday nights at the Conneaut Elks Lodge for 25 years. He only had one drink in his life at his wedding celebration in 1967, at St. Joseph Catholic Church in Ashtabula, Ohio. John married Emily Frances Carroll, a second-generation elementary schoolteacher who was in her own right good-hearted, creative, generous, and well-loved.

They began our family by adopting me, then bore three sons. Nothing, in our eyes, could ever surpass his distinguishment as our beloved father: good natured, kind, compassionate, honest, moral, fair, hardworking, humorous. My father connected us to the world in many ways. One of those was through his love of language.

I know he spoke at least five languages besides English: Dutch, German, Frisian, Afrikaans, and Spanish. This self-taught linguist may have been fluent in more, but his modesty and unassuming nature prevents us from knowing the full extent. I once tried to trip him up by greeting him with Japanese: Konnichiwa. He didn't miss a beat, but responded, "It's Kon-ee-chee-wah, no emphasis on any syllable."

At our house, it was literally as common to discuss language as it was football. Our family was accustomed to the image of my father with books and flashcards; he created volumes of flashcards, with phrases in languages such as Spanish and Afrikaans on one side, and their English translations on the other. He kept stacks of them, written by hand on ruled index cards and bound with rubber bands, near his recliner. He would hold them on his lap and flip through them, murmuring the

Flashcards from the collection

foreign sentences while the television was on (always go from the English side to the foreign side). He carried them with him in public, and while he stood in lines or sat in waiting rooms, he would pull out the cards, silently reading them and flipping them over to check the translations. He would affectionately greet us children and call us by our names in Esperanto, Spanish, or German, teach us little songs in Esperanto, and holiday greetings in various languages. He and I would walk through the nearby cemetery and read the names aloud; he would identify their origins and make the proper pronunciation accordingly.

He was a language-based visionary and Futurist. How progressive was it that in the 1950s, fresh out of college, he relocated to Mexico to live with a host family for one year, in order to learn the Spanish language! Spanish has become the second language of the U.S. since then. Whenever my father encountered native Spanish speakers, he warmly engaged them with flawless, accent-free Spanish, all to their delight. Thus, he maintained friendships with people of various ages and backgrounds, because of the bridges he built through language.

But natural languages are created by tribes within borders, and thus limit the possibilities for boundless human communication. Enter constructed languages.

He became enamored of the opportunities offered by international language. He was involved with the constructed, or artificial, languages (called "conlangs" within this special interest linguistic community) of Esperanto, Lingua Franca Nova, and Nordienisk.

Rick Harrison, editor of the magazine *Journal of Planned Languages* (and creator of the language Vorlin), is credited with explaining artificial languages this way:

"An artificial language is a language that has been deliberately designed by one person or a small group of people over a relatively short period of time.

Synonyms for the term artificial language include planned language, constructed language, model language, and invented language. Artificial languages designed for specific purposes are also known by an array of other terms. Those used in works of fiction are called imaginary languages or fictional languages. Those designed to facilitate global communications are called universal languages, auxiliary languages (auxlangs), interlanguages or interlinguas, international languages, etc. The realm of artificial languages also includes logical languages, number languages, symbolic languages a.k.a. icon(ic) languages, and pasimologies (gesture languages)," (Harrison's definition appears on *The Essential Travel Phrases* website.)

"Some of these languages have had more visibility than others: Esperanto, Star Trek's Klingon, Tolkien's Quenya, Lojban, and Volapük are some examples," (David McCreedy extrapolated on his Travel Phrases website.)

Language is the foundation of successful civilizations. My father was involved in the flagship artificial language of "Esperanto, the international language," for forty years. Esperanto appealed to him not simply as a straightforward, cleanly constructed language, but as the means toward a new way of living on earth. The vision of Esperanto was philosophical: to provide a way for all people to communicate with one another, regardless of their native language(s), anywhere on earth. As he explained to me during my childhood Esperanto lessons - if you learned Esperanto, you could go anywhere in the world and find someone wearing a green star, and the two of you could speak together. What a beautiful idea.

He outgrew Esperanto as its popularity waned, and more attractive alternative language projects became visible.

"Classic Esperanto is hard to pronounce and has too many phonemes, but it will never change. There are a zillion "esperantidos" out there, but they're voices crying in the wilderness," he wrote.

But for all of my father's embracing of foreign languages, his first love was Old English.

He asserted that English is a Germanic language. Generations of students in his English classes in Jefferson High School learned to recognize the roots of their mother tongue, and took on the corrective phrase, "That's unEnglish!" He would point out true English words in daily speech with a gladdened heart, and could easily identify the origin of words when asked. He and I would sing the song Edelweiss, and he would always light up and say, "Every word in the song is pure English, except for the title."

Thus his personal language project evolved.

"In my early adulthood, I began toying with the idea of re-Germanizing the English language," he wrote.

The premise was a small, but consequential, hypothetical tweaking of an historical event.

In 1066, William I, King of Normandy, sailed with his army across the English Channel and attacked the armies of King Harold in the coastal town of Hastings, England. The battle began early on the morning of

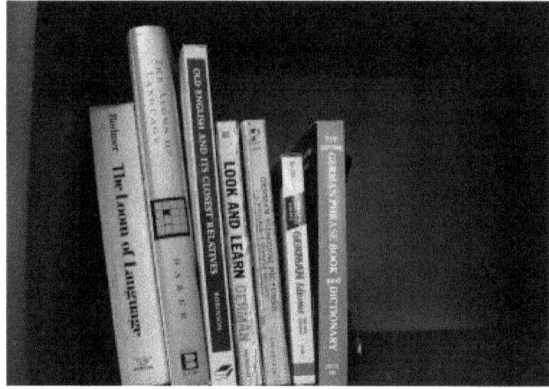

Favored reference books

October 14, 1066. It surged back and forth as the afternoon wore on, with one side, and then the other, appearing to gain temporary advantage. But late in the day, King Harold died. Legend has it that he fell from his horse, pierced through the eye by a Norman arrow. Despairing from the loss of their leader, the English armies retreated, and William installed himself as King of England. William became forever known as William the Conqueror.

For the next three hundred years, French was the language of the court and of the ruling French aristocracy in England. Before 1066, the commonfolk in England—the peasants and farmers—spoke a form of Anglo-Saxon now known as Old English. But over the three centuries after King Harold's defeat at the Battle of Hastings, French words and phrases infiltrated—some would say corrupted, and others would say enhanced—the English language. As a result, Modern English evolved from a blending of French and Anglo-Saxon Old English. To this day, if an English speaker wants to appear officious or imperious, they can employ English words of French derivation (e.g., officious, imperious, derivation). But if an English speaker wants to sound like salt of the earth, they can use English words that came from Anglo-Saxon (e.g., salt, earth, came.)

So, my father wondered, what if, late in the afternoon of October 14, 1066, that Norman arrow had missed King Harold? What if Harold's armies had won the day and repelled William and his Norman army from England? What if Anglo-Saxon had continued evolving on its own, without being inundated over the following centuries by tens of thousands of French words?

"I started out with the insane idea that I could determine what the English language would be like today if the English had defeated the Normans at the Battle of Hastings, October 14, 1066!" he wrote. "When I realized that I was in over my head, I scaled down my ambition to re-Germanizing the English language. Even that is a lofty goal."

Thus, he narrowed his focus.

"I then decided on a more modest project, the creation of a Germanic dialect favoring West Germanic (English, Frisian, Flemish, Dutch, Afrikaans, Plattdeutsch) and North Germanic (Icelandic, Swedish, Norwegian, Danish). The term Low German is used by some linguists to designate the West Germanic languages. Although my created dialect and English have a common origin, it is not English. It is, rather, a Pan-Germanic language."

He called his conlang Saksen (alternate spellings which exist in his notes include Sacsen, Saxon and Saxen). For him, working on Sasken was both an exercise in applying his knowledge and linguistic logic, as well as a satisfying creative outlet for aesthetics and experimentation.

Correspondence from longtime Estonian penpal

"Two of the most eyecatching spellings of Saksen are the double *aa* and the use of the vowel combinations *ae*, *ie*, *ou*, *ouw*, *oe*, *oew*, *ue*, and *uew*," he wrote.

It is my hope that not only will linguists and conlangers admire this constructed language called Saksen, but also that a wider spectrum of readers, regardless of familiarity with linguistics, can thumb through this Saksen vocabulary and appreciate its depth, rhythm, and art, as well as its Germanic allusions.

As the digital and informational ages rose in the 1990s and 2000s, so did the world of constructed languages. Persons scattered around the globe, working on independent conlang projects, now had a means to communicate and collaborate, through online forums, wikis, blogs, groups, over Twitter and Facebook; conlangers began to converge on basically every emerging communication platform on the World Wide Web. As a Futurist, my father was enthralled by this movement. The man who had maintained bilingual relationships with penpals in other countries for years now participated in the conlang section of the Essential Travel Phrases website (www.travelphrases.info). He struck up an ongoing email correspondence with the now-late secretary of the United States/ American Interlingua Society, Paul LeCorde, of Kentucky (Paul May). Paul and my father, who were 31 years and two states apart, bridged a friendship through sharing their respective conlang projects (LeCorde's project was Nordienisk/ Neuorndien).

In 2011, he wrote to Paul that a Germanic auxlang is what really interested him.

My father considered Saksen his hobby. He certainly did not write it for academic publication nor professional recognition. He did not intend for it to become a widely used language. In fact, there were few he shared it with. He shrugged off my notion to publish his dictionary, and even to have it exist in print. It is therefore important to note that this edition is not as he intended for publication and is not polished; I assembled this by rescue and recovery of his material posthumously, with greathearted help from those named in the acknowledgments section, to whom I am deeply grateful. So not all of his manuscript was available (only his notes of corrections represent the vocabulary lists of letters J through O), and it cannot be known exactly how he would have presented it. I expect that if my father were presented with this hard copy of his dictionary today, he would laugh modestly and downplay the importance of his project. Then he would steadily, quietly, and contentedly go about the neverending task of editing it.

It is true that his purpose behind creating Saksen was not to deliver to the world a superior, working, artificial language. It was not created with any idea of recognition at all. In fact, it was not even created with the idea that you would be reading it over right now. Rather, creating his own language was a pure, personal, labor of love which naturally evolved from the burning creativity, intellect, and independently-pursued education of a brilliant man. In these pages, as in life, John C. Ricker provides us a transcendent, timeless bridge to humanity, which he held so dear.

"We are Oracles. Seers. We are Bridges and Beacons. We are Conlangers."

—*attributed to Thaenn on the* FrathWiki *website*

ACKNOWLEDGMENTS

THE FOLLOWING PERSONS contributed to the recovery of these materials:
Jon Ricker
Tom Ricker
Patrick Dobbins
Paul Bierly
Nathan Burcham
Robert Colyar
Paul LeCorde (May)
Darla Schanfish

SPECIAL THANKS TO:
Paul Bierly
Jamie Sinnott

Part 1

Saksen Explained

INTRODUCTION

What Saksen is

ENGLISH IS A Germanic language, but the number of words of English origin in the language is only around 25 percent. The English people became enamored of French and Latin and jettisoned their native vocabulary. After learning some German and Dutch, I realized that even common expressions in English employ French and Latin words. It was then, in my early adulthood, that I began toying with the idea of re-Germanizing the English language.

I began creating words to replace borrowed words using native word stock (for example, thoughtgift for suggestion). Although this idea produced some neat words, it did not make possible the re-Germanizing of the language. There were simply not enough English words in the dictionary to accomplish the task.

I then asked myself this question: If the English had won the Battle of Hastings, what would the language be like today? After entertaining the idea for some time, I realized that I lacked the competence to approach the re-Germanizing of the language in that way. Besides, some smart alec from the University of Chicago with a degree in Germanic philology could gleefully tear it apart. When I realized that I was in over my head, I scaled down my ambition to re-germanisizing the English language. Even that is a lofty goal.

So I then decided on a more modest project, the creation of a Germanic dialect favoring West Germanic (English, Frisian, Flemish, Dutch, Afrikaans, Plattdeutsch) and North Germanic (Icelandic, Swedish, Norwegian, Danish). The term Low German is used by some linguists to designate the West Germanic languages.

I decided to use Dutch as my control language even though English is a West Germanic language and not a dialect of Low German. Frisian is West Germanic, but I can't find enough material on it, and it has a lot of dialects. I'm also using German, Afrikaans, Norwegian (Bokmal dialect), and the limited amount of

Frisian that I have. Of course, Old and Modern English are also used. Generally I respelled Modern English words of Germanic origin to fit my spelling system. I did the same with words I borrowed from the other Germanic languages and words taken from Latin and Latin through French. If German borrowed a French or Latin word, I usually accepted it. Dutch verbs are pretty tricky if they have prefixes. Sometimes the prefix is separable when the verb is conjugated, and sometimes it isn't. For example, aanbreken becomes breek aan when conjugated. On the other hand, in the word aanbrengen, the prefix is not separated when the verb is conjugated. German also has separable prefixes. English lacks this phenomenon.

Although my created dialect and English have a common origin, it is not English. It is, rather, a Pan-Germanic language.

–John C. Ricker
Ashtabula, Ohio
1936–2018

Al due bie meyliig.
(All is possible.)

SPELLING

1. I eliminated double (twin) consonants except to preserve a closed syllable. This is what is done in Dutch. Double consonants are pronounced as one as in German and Dutch. They can only occur after **single vowel letters:** *academmish, ecumennish,* Words ending in single consonants:
   hal, hac, (but *backing* if -ing is added), *hil (but hilZig* when -ig is added).

2. c-, -c, -ck
   C precedes back vowels (a, o, u): *cat, cot, cut,* It also precedes consonants:
   cliever.
   C follows a single vowel letter: *fric, loc, hac, luc*
   K precedes front vowels (i, e) and also y: *kiep, kiel, keg, kyser.*
   K also follows consonants: *bank, drink,foelk.*
   K also follows two vowel letters andy: *misteik, buek, luek, lyk*

3. This is my most stringent rule, and one that has caused me a lot of problems: the vowel letters a, e, i, o, u cannot end a primary stress syllable.
   Primary stress syllables can end in these vowels (all long or actual diphthongs): *aa, ei, ie, oe, ou, ue, y.*
   Primary stress syllables can also end in a closed syllable.
   (closed syllables) *abac, ankel, baarmeid, middel*
   (open syllables) *daatum, ferdyting +, hoelig, gruesum, hieden, housing,*
   +fer always has weak stress and is slurred.
   As can be seen, closed syllables can have both long and short vowels.

4. *aa, aaw, ei, ie, oe, oew, ou, ouw, ue, uew*
   aa, ei, oe, ou, ue can end syllables but not words.

ie can end a syllable as well as a word. (There are exceptions for function words.)

Examples: *faader, oefrig, ji·uetig, pouder* (syllables)

laaw, trouw, truew (words)

W is also required to separate the double vowel letters from another vowel: *touwel; frouwen, trouwen, bluewel; moewer*

PRONUNCIATION

The following consonants are pronounced approximately as in Modern English: *b, ch, dg, h, j, k, l, m, n, p, v.*

Special attention must be paid to the following:

c always like /k/

d and *t* (tip of tongue must be against back of upper teeth. Never pronounced like din **ready** or tin **city.**) *d = t* after *n* (**hand**)

g always pronounced as in **get** and **tag.** Never pronouned like the *g* in **general.**

-ng like the *-ng* in **ring,** Never like the *-ng* in **linger**

r (tip of tongue against the ridge of the upper teeth.) This sound is spelled *tt, t, dd, d* in weakly stressed syllables in Modern English: *city, latter.,, ladde1; ready.* It will take some practice to learn to start a word with this sound. (Pretend you're a kid making the sound of a toy truck.)

s (like the *s* in **soft,** the double *s* in **less.** (Some speakers will tend to pronounce it as /zl, especially between vowels. As the plural ending for nouns, it is pronounced /zl after voiced consonants: **legs, fueds, livs, robs**

w is pronounced as /v/ at the beginning of words.

After the consonants, *c, d, t, like !wl:* **swetter, dwell, twin, cwelle**

It is silent in these combinations: *aaw, oew, ouw, uew*

w is also silent before *r: wrist, wring, wryte z* is pronounced *Its/* after n: danz (dance). Elsewhere *z* is pronounced as in Modern English.

+ *ch, tch, dg,* and *sh* are pronounced as in ME.

+ *ch* starts words and syllables and follows consonants and double vowels

+ *tch* ends closed syllables after single vowel letters

Vowels and Dipthongs

One characteristic of Germanic languages is the distinction between long and short vowels. Vowel length distinguishes words.

Short

a (like the *aw* in law)

Long

aa (like the *a* in father)

e (like the *e* in bet)

e like the *e* in mother (schwa)

ei (like the *a* in mate, the *ey* in obey, they)

i (like the *i* in hit-closed syllable)

ie (like they in happy in open syllable, median stress)

(i cannot end a common word or come before *r* if *r* ends a closed syllable)

(like the *ea* in heat, the *ee* in see)

(like they in happy at the end of a word)

o (like the *o* in gonna, ford)

oe(w) (like the *o* in go, hold; *oe* ends a syllable; *oew* ends a word)

u (like the *u* in put-closed syllable primary stress)

(like the *oo* in washroom in closed syllable, median stress).

ue(w) (like the *ue* in blue, the *ew* in stew; *ue* ends a syllable; *uew* ends a word)

y (like the yin by, the i in kite) (like they in you at the be ginning of words)

ou(w) (like the *ow* in how, the *ou* in **shout;** *ou* ends a syllable; *ouw* ends a word.)

GRAMMAR: PART 1

Noun Plurals

-S after vowels or single consonants
(beds, rags, hats, religgens, alpaacas)

+ -EN after two or three consonants, after *ch, dg, sh, tch, s, z*
(danzen, horsen, daarten, hindernessen, baasen, biechen, wishen, frenden, batchen.)

+ Words ending in *-ng* may use either suffix. **(rings, ringen)**

Verbs

Saksen has two infinitives:

1. The E-infinitive (the one listed in the dictionary)
   duewe (do), *fragge* (ask), *telle* (tell, count)
   This infinitive follows modals and the preposition *tue.*
2. The EN-infinitive (not listed in the dictionary) This infinitive is the same as the gerund in ME. It can follow any preposition except *tue.*
3. Present tense consists of *due + the E-infinitive:*
   Ic due sie dit. (I see it.) This form also covers the present progressive and the emphatic present tenses.
4. Past tense consists of *did + the E-infinitive.*
   Ic did sie die film This fonn also covers past progressive and emphatic past.
5. Future tense consists of *wil+ the E-infinitive.*
   Ic wilsie die film leiter dis wiek. (I'll see the movie later this week.)
6. As in ME *wil* does not have to be used if future time is implied (especially in subordinate clauses):
   Wie can miete after yue (due) ende wurk.
   + *Due* can be left out at the discretion of the user.

7. The mood tenses are covered by the following modals:
   can-cud, wil-wud, shud (Sal is not used J, *wit tue (=want),*
   mey-myt, must

GRAMMAR: PART 2

These verbs are considered *defective* because they lack infinitive *forms*.

I. Only the following verbs can carry tense (show time):

Verb (infinitive)	Present	Past
duewe	duew	did
havve (tue) +	hav	had
shalle	shall*	shud
wille ++	will	wud
wille tue **	wille tue	wud tue
canne	can	cud
musse	muss	must
otte (tue)	ot	ot
maye	may	miet

+ **Havve** carries tense only when used as an auxiliary.

* Shall is not used in popular speech.

++ **Wille** when followed by an infinitive either indicates the future or suggests determination.

** **Wille tue** when followed by an infinitive means *want to*.

II. Saksen has two infinitive forms:

A. The *e*-infinitive corresponds to the English infinitive. The *E* is mute. Its only purpose is to indicate that the word so suffixed is an infinitive. It is often preceded by *tue*. After the modal auxiliaries *tue* does not occur:

Ick can helpe yue after weurk.

Ick did cuepe oen nuew caar.

13

B. The **en**-infinitive corresponds to the English gerund. It often follows prepositions (except **tue**):

Ick did biede hoem insted av goewen tue dee gaem.

The **en**-infinitive also occurs in subject or object positions independent of a preposition and is often interchangeable with **tue** + an **e**-infinitive.

Tue goewe nouw duew maeke noe sens.

Goewen nouw duew maeke noe sens.

III. Here are a few differences between Saksen and English spelling and pronunciation:

A. The vowel letters a,e,i,o, and u cannot end a stressed syllable unless the word has only one syllable:

capell (cah PEL)
beseeke (buh SEEK)
me (MEE)
tofrid (to FRID)
ya (YAH)

B. The suffix **e**, which only occurs with the **e**-infinitive, does not affect the pronunciation of any preceding vowels of the infinitive:

ferweurdige (fuhr WUHR dig)
gaddere (GAH duhr)
misberre (mis BAIR)

C. Stressed syllables can be closed or open. Open syllables that are stressed will contain more than one vowel letter. Closed syllables that are stressed can contain either one vowel letter or two or three. When the combination -**er** occurs in a syllable, that syllable can never be stressed.

ablaes (ah BLYZ)
becwaam (buh CWAHM)
couwbaarn (COW bahrn)
feroening (fuhr OH ning)
masheen (mah SHEEN)
nuews (nooz)
saamling (SAHM ling)
seckerness (SECK uhr ness)

D. Words which end in unstressed *-en*, *-el*, or *-er* lose a syllable if a suffix beginning with a vowel is added. This same phenomenon occurs in spoken English but is usually not accompanied by a spelling change.

> **gaddere + ing = gaddring**
> **heere + er = heerder (The d is added for ease of pronunciation.)**
> **reckene = er = reckner**
> **saamele + ing = saamling**

Note that double consonants, if they occur, are not simplified.

E. Two of the most eyecatching spellings of Sakson are the double *aa* and the use of the vowel combinations *ae, ie, ou, ouw, oe, oew, ue,* and *uew*. The syllables in which they occur receive either primary stress or median stress, usually the former. *Y* is found usually at the ends of words or before another vowel: *fyer, by*. It is a dipthong made up of the sounds *ah* + *ee* and is pronounced exactly the same as the *y* in English *by*.

F. The English firstperson pronoun *I* is *ick* in Saksen.

PHRASES

Earthquakes are very common in California.	Errtcweiks due bie bissen gemein in California.
Did John leave?	Did Yoehaan lieve?
They're on good terms with each other.	Dey due bie aan gued terrms mecaar (mid iechander).
We don't have air-conditioning.	Wie duenie havve climatiserring.
I don't like to take sides.	Ic duenie lyke tue teike syds.
I took the dog for a walk.	Ic did teike die hund for yn waak.
I caught a cold.	Ic did fange yn coeld.
I hung up my clothes.	Ic did hange up my claddingen. (claddings)
Prices have gone up.	Prysen did goewe up.
I'm sorry to intrude.	Ic due bie saarig tue breike in aan yue.
He had an accident.	Hie did havve yn infal (mishap).
I didn't want to attract attention.	Ic dienie wille tue trecke aan bemaarking.

We changed clothes.	Wie did ferandere claddingen (claddings).
I have many responsibilities.	Ic due havve mennig anserlignessen.
We got tired of waiting.	Wie did tyere av weiten.
The foreigners always stick together.	Die fremders(fremdlanders) altyd blye tuegedder (saamen).
The visitor asked for directions.	Die besieker did fragge im wysingen.
Where is my room?	Werr due bie my ruem?
Where is the beach?	Werr due bie die strand?
Where is the bar?	Werr due bie die baar?
Don't touch me there!	Doent aanruere mie derr.
He looks very healthy.	Hie due lueke bissen heltig(gesund).
I heard that it is true.	Ic did hiere dat it due bie truew(waar).
Never in my life was I so angry.	Nevver in my lyf did ic bie soew angrig(tornig).
I don't know where to look.	Ic duenie witte werr tue lueke.
When I was twelve years old, we moved to Ohio.	Wen ic did bie twelv yiers oeld, wie did beweye tue Ohyow.
I didn't buy it because it was too expensive.	Ic dienie cuepe dit fordat it did bie tue costlig (dier).
We can't get used to it.	Wie cannie gette bewoend tue dit (it).

I can't get along without my coffee in the morning.	Ic cannie gette alang sonder my coffie in die morgen.
She gets along with everyone.	She due gette alang mid allen.
He gave up smoking.	Hie did givve up smoken (or smoken up).
She needs an operation.	Shie due niede yn operaasen.
It's hard for us to imagine it.	It due bie swierig for us tue ferbelde dit.
He wasted a lot of money.	Hie did fercwiste (misbrueke) mutch (bissen) geld.
We had to sell it at a loss.	Wie did havve tue selle (fercuepe) dit at yn los.
It seems impossible.	It due sieme unmeylig.
All is possible.	Al due bie meyliig.

SAMPLE

TRANSLATION OF AN article from the *Star Beacon* newspaper, Ashtabula, Ohio

Gletcher Landwied Paark

Dee twistend roeds av Gletcher Landwied Paark, Montaana, duew givve tuerists oen undergang av oen lieftied at eefrig tum.

Oen cwick ress true dee paark for oen week av camping under dee oepen hevvens duew ferhavve sheen landscaeps, mutch wieldlief, en missenlitch gelayennesses tue fange natuer on film.

My ress in dee summer of 2001 tue Gletcher Landwied Paark did be deel av oen lang ress av 1, 8660 miels in twee lands witch did laste six days. It did slisse in deels av Waashington, Iedahoew, Montaana, Brittish Columbia, en Albeurta.

Camping at Gletcher Landwied Paark duew wrappe in plannen abed tue gette bespeekings for fittend campsteds, maar oen dayress true dee paark duew lende moer bendsumness.

Oen oentiedfee, witch duew oepene oen mennigness av gelayenesses, duew undersheede frum boeten tue mueswaachen tue fangen dee perrfect sunset. Dee Roed tue dee Sun, oen bekenned switchback driev true dee paark, duew offere oen brettaekend siet av dee paark, witch duew beginne at Ioew raesings en duew riese tue graet hiets at dee ander end av dee paark.

Tue ferseeke tue beseeke sutch oen graet bedraag(bredt) av ground in sutch oen short tied did meene dat my beseek tue dee paark wud Iaste oenlig neer fiev stunds(tieds). Dat did meen dat ick must runne frum oen sied av dee paark tue dee ander in hoeps av fangen oen foetoew av dee perrfect sunset.

Dee feurst hindring tue diss weurlwund tuer did be oen waatrig landdeel mennig miels frum dee ingang tue dee paark, werr oen graet gruep av tuerists had gaddered. Ick did finde oen sted tue paarke en did runne back mid my cammeras. Ick did finde mennig graet mues, witch did underhoelde mennig happig beseekers.

Dee ried true dee twistend, bendend roeds av dee paark did at last leede me tue chuese between de folgend: reeche Calgary, Al beurta befoer 1 bmd. or fange dee sunset oever dee berrgentops. Alltied Iueken for undernieming, ick did chuese dee latter and did sherre dee sunset mid twee berrgengoets. Dee paark duew be oen sted dat ick will nevllt -fergette, en ick duew hoepe tue goewe back. Oen neerder sted av bestemming for dee tweed day wud seeme tue be oen gued idee.

—*Warren Dillaway,*
Staarbeeken Staffwrieter

Part 2

Saksen Dictionary

a

a, an
yn

aback
aback

abaft
abaft

abandon
lieve (behind) fersaeke ferlette

abase
ferneddere

abate
lette up, lessene

abatement
lessning, fermindring

abatoir
slaaterhous

abbess
hedsister

abbey
sisterhous, sisteraboed

abbot
hedbrueder

abbreviate
shortene, fershorte

abbreviation
shortning, fershorting

abdicate
givve up, lieve, yelde, stande doun

abdication
dounstand, sietyelding

abdomen
maaw, belgen

abduct
unfuere, kidnappe. stiele

abductor
unfuerder, kidnapper

abduction
unfuering, kidnapping

aberrant
mindwaandrend

aberation
mindwaanderness

abet
helpe, ferlende

abettor
helper, ferlender

abeyance
tydlig halt, tydligness unlastinghalt

abhor
haete, loede

abhorrence
haet, loeding

abide
abyde

abiding
abydend

ability
fermayenness, becwaamness

abject
oeveraarm, wretched, hienlig

abjure
unsaye, ferswerre

abjuration
unsaying, ferswerring

ablative
(gram.) ablativ

ablaze
aflaem, in flaems, ablaes

(be) able (to)
fermaye, canne

able
becwaam, fermayen

-able(suffix) -
baar

able-bodied -
fullcrafted, strong, heltig

abnegate
givve up, bestryte self

abnegation
selfbestryt, selffernoewing

abnormal
unbewoenlig, abnormall

abnormality
unbewoenligness

aboard
abord, on bord

abode
aboed, woening, dwelling

abolish
duewe away mid, offshaffe, ferduewe

abolition
offshaffing, ferdied

abominable
haetful, dredful, loedend

abominate
ferloede, ferhaete, ferdredde

aboriginal
(adj) inborn, hierborn

aborigine
inbornling

abort
unferblueme, misberre, maeke faelburt

abortion
unferblueming, misberring, faelburt

abortive
unferbluemig, misberrig, unwastemberrig, wastemless, fruetless

abound
oeverfloewe mid, tieme mid, bie floewend(ritch), mid (in)

abounding
oeverfloewend, tiemend

about
about, arund, (prefix) im-

above
boeven, abuev, upsterrs, upway

abreast
abrest

abridge
abridge, shortene
fershorte

abridgement
abridging, shortning fershorting

abrupt
cwickbraekend, cwickhaltend
cwickstaapend

abscond
maeke av mid
stiele av (away) mid

absent
offwessend,missend
unhierig

abscess
puss-swelling

abstain
hoelde back av unbestemme

abstention
backhoelding, stem- hoelding, unbestemming

abstinence
backhoeldness, unbestemness

abstract
(adj) unfremd, unwend, ununderstandig, unferstandig (n) abstract

abstraction
unfremding, unwend- ing, ununderstand, unferstand

abundant
oeverfloewend, ferfull, (bie) nytsum

absurd
oeverdum

abuse
(v) misbrueke, illbrueke (n) edwit, misbruek, illbruek

abusive
misbruekend, illbruekend

abut
(vi) grense (aan) (vt) belende

abutment
belending

abyss
newellness

academic
academmish

academy
academmie

accelerate
fercwicke, bespiede, fersnelle

acceleration
fercwicking, bespied- ing, fersnelling

accelerator
bespieder, fersneller

accent
(v) betoene, bewaye (n) betoening, ferbewaying, acsent, spiechway

accentuate
betoene

accept
aannyme, acsepterre

acceptance
aannym

access
(n) tuegang, upwelling

accessible
tueganglig

accessibility
tuegangligness

accession
rys, upgang

accident
mishap, unfall (chance event) tuefall

accidental
tuefallig

acclaim
haele

acclamation
byfall

acclimatize
beclyme
aclymaterre

accolade
acolaad

accommodate
befitte, passe aan

accommodation
befitting, aanpassing

accompaniment
belieding

accompanist
belieder

accompany
goewe mid, beliede, bie led by, beliede ynself aan

accomplice
helper (prefix) mid - , fellow -

accomplish
fullende, ferfulle, geduewe

accomplishment
fullend, died, genordness

accord
ynmindedness, oeveryncuemst, oeverynstemming

accordance
oeverynstemming

according to
after, faalowend, (var.) foelgend, foelgens

accordion
acordien

account
(n. report) beryt, fertelling (com.)
geroed,reckning

(on) ____(of)
aan fruemer av

(take into)_____
(taeke, nyme) intue reckning

account (for)
fercliere av, ansere for

accountable
anserig

accounting

buekkeeping

accouterments
geraed

accredit
betruste

accreditation
betrust

accumulate
hiepe

accumulation
hiep

accuracy
rytigness

accurate
rytig

accursed
werrger, fersworn, bewaarigd

accusation
beshuldiging, aanclaag, betyting

accusative
(gram.) acuesativ

accusatory
beshuldigend

accuse
beshuldige, aanclaage

accuser
beshuldiger, aanclaager

accustom (onesself)
bewoene self tue

accustomed
bie bewoen tue

ace
aes

ache
(v) aeke , smaarte (n) aek, paen

achieve
fullende, fullbringe

achievement
fullending, fullbringen

acknowledge
bekenne, andette, (receipt) beryte

acknowledgment
bekentness, andetting, (receipt) beryt

acoustic
acuestic, ferhierig

acoustics
acuestics

acquaint
maeke bekent

acquaintance
bekentness, (a person) bekender

acquire
bestriene, gette, beoewne

acquisition
(thing) bestriening, beoewning (act of)
bestrienen,
beoewnen

acquit
unbeshuldige, unbegiltige

acquittal
unbeshuldiging, unbegiltiging

acre
aeker

across
oever, across

act
(v) duewe,handele, benyme, maeke believe,
(play) ferplaye (n) died,(play) act, die
Handelings av die Apostels(Cristfoelgers)

acting
ferplaying beliefmaeking

active
bedryvig, weurksum

activity
bedryvigness

actor
ferplayer, shoewplayer

act upon
wurke aan, maeke died
mid

actual(ly)
wurklig

actuality
wurkligness

acute
sharp, kien, hevvig

adapt
bewurke, beaarbyde

adaptation
bewurking, beaarbyding

add
(math) telle up, adde tue, fermoere

addition
(math) uptelling adding, fermoering

address
(n) adress,, maelsted, spiech (v)
adresse(envelope) spieke tue

adequacy
fulldiedness

adequate

fullduen

adhere
sticke tue, faalowe, foelge, clieve tue, hoelde
tue

adherence
clieving , hoelding

adherent
faalower, foelger
fellow--

adhesion
adhessen

adhesive
(n) clieving, cliever (adj)clievend

adjacent
aangrensend,
nierby

adjourn
ferdaye

adjournment
ferdaying

adjunct
add-aan

adjure
beswerre

adjuration
beswerring

adjust
befitte, bringe in order,
regulerre, aanpasse

adjustment
befitting, aanpassing,
regulerring

administer
beherre, bestiere

administration
beherr, bestier

administrative
beherrish, bestierish

administrator
beherrder,bestierder

admirable
bewunderbaar

admiration
bewundring, feroering

admire
bewundere, feroere, lueke up tue

admissability
inletbaarness, andetbaarness admissable
inletbaar, andetbaar admit
andette, lette in (pop.) fesse up

admixture
blend

ado
aduew

adopt
nyme oever, taeke for yns oewn

adoption
oevernyming

adoptive
oevernymen

adore
wurshippe

adoration
wurship

adorn
bedecke, glenge

adornment
bedecking

adult
fullgroewn, groewnup,
fullwaxen

adulterate
ferfalsse, maeke under-
wurtig,
ferunderwurte

adulterer
wedlaakbraeker

adultery
wedlaakbraek

advance
goewe foerway, befoerdere

advancement

befoerdring

advantage
ferdiel, foerluck,
foerhelp

advantageous
foerluckig, foerhelpish

advent
hiddercueming (rel.) Foercristburttyd, Advent

adventure
(n) undernyming, plie, derring (v) waye

adventurous
derringbent, ferwayen

adverb
(gram.) adverb,

imstandwurd

adversary
foew, widstander. unfrend, gewinner

adverse
widdrig, (weather)
swierig

advertise
behiede, adverterre,
anonserre, selltaake

advertisement
behied, saelcall,
fercuepcall,
reclaam, anonsing

advertising
behieding

advice
raad

advise
raadde, givve raad tue

advocate
(n) laawcrafter,
laawwitter (v) spieke for

advocacy
forspiech

aerial
(cmpnd) luft- (adj) luftig (n) antenna

afar
afaar

affair
ferwryting, sack(matter) (amorous)
luevsack,aferr

affect
swaye, befiele, beruere

affectation
waarmt, haartlykness

affectionate
waarm, haartlyk

affirm
ferseckere

affirmation
ferseckring

affirmative
beyaahend, (**answer in the __-_**) beyaahende

afflict
beswende, hyne,
swenche

affliction
beswend, swench

affluent
ritch, weltig

affluence
ritchness, weltigness

afford
aforde, havve die geld
for

afield
afeld

afoot
afuet

afraid
bang, (be) _____ (of): (bie) bang (av or for)

Africa
Africa

African
(adj) Africannish (n) Africanner

after
after

aftermath
aftermat

afternoon
aftermidday

afterward(s)
aftertyd, laeter

again
agen, anuew, afresh, eft (prefix) ed-, nuew-,
back

against
wid, taegen

age
(length of life) alder, livtyd, oeldness (period of
time) tyds, erra

agency
bemidling

agent
handler, bemidler

aggravate
ferwurse, wursene

aggravation
ferwursing, wursning

aggression
aanfall

aggressive
aanfallig

agressiveness
aanfalligness

ago
agoew. befoer, back (fol-
lowing a time word)

agonize
struggele mid smaart(paen)

agonizing
strugglend

agony
smaartsstruggel, soelsmaarts, soelpaen
detpangs

agree

bedwerre,
stemme oeveryn, bie av yn mind(stem)

agreeable
(weather) angenaem, (willing to agree)-
ynmindig, av yn mind agreement
oeverynstemming, ynmindness, bedwerring

agriculture
landtilling

agricultural
landtillish

aground
agrund

ahead
ahed

aid
(n) help, gefilsten

(v) helpe, fulltumme first-aid
- fursthelp

aide
helper, fulltummer

ail
bie sick (ill)

ailment
sickness, illness

aim
(v) (taeke) aim (at)- tiele aan, taeke duel at (n) goel, wish, duel

air (n)
luft (v) bespieke, saye out

airplane
luftcraft, flycraft

airy
luftig, windig

ajar
ajaar, slytlig oepen

akin
akin

alarm
(n) alaarm, waarning, fier (v) alaarme, waarne

alarm clock
waeker

alarming
befierend, befrytend

alcohol
alcohoel

alcoholic
(adj) alcohoelish, (n) alcohoeliker

alcoholism
alcohoelishness

alder
alder

alderman
alderman, alderwyt

ale
ael

alert
awaek, waeksum, aan die luekout waachful

alertness
waeksumness, waachfulness

alien
(a) fremd, unerrtlig (n) fremder, fremdling, unerrtliger, outlander

alienate
befremde

alienation

befremdness

alight from
alyte av, styge out, steppe out, steppe doun av

alike
alyk

alive
alyv, livvend

all
(prn--everything) aller (prn--everyone) aller (prefix) all- (adj) all

allegation
bewerring

allege
bewerre

allegorical
allegorrish

allegory
allegorrie

allergic
allergish

allergy
allergie

alleviate
suede, fermilde, lessene , lytene

alley

stieg, naarowway,
strietling

allegiance
trouwness

alliance
ferbond

allot
ferdiele

allotment
ferdieling

allow
givve s.y. liev tue, ferlieve, getaffe, lette

allowable
ferleft

allowance
(money) tydgeld

allowances
ferlievings

alloy
blending

all-around
allarund, allsydig

All Saints' Day
Allhoeligsday

allude (to)
hinte (at)

allure
besnerre, ferlaake

alluring
besnerrish, ferlaakish

allurement
besnerring, ferlaaking

allusion
hint, mieningplay, aanspieding

alliance
ferbond

ally
(n) boelsterder, boelsterfrend, midkemper (v)
ferbinde

almighty

allmytig,
die Allmytig(Herr)

almond
mandel

almost
allmoest, nier, ny, nierlig

alms
aarmengift, almues

alms-house
aarmenhous

aloft
aluft

alone
alyn (let ___) lette alyn

along
alang

aloof
aluef

aloud
aloud

alphabet

alfabet

already

allreddig

alright
allryt

also
allsoew

altar
wiefod, wybed, hoelig boerd, alter

alter
ferandere

alteration
ferandring

alternate
(v) ferwende, taeke ferwendings (or burts)
(adj) ferwendish (n) stedtaeker, stednymer

alternative
ferwending, burtling

although
aldoe

altitude
hyt, hyness

alto

altow

altogether
alltuegedder,saemtydlig

alum
alum

aluminum
alueminum

always
alltyd, immer. simmel

a.m.(A.M.)
fmd.(foermidday)

amateur
amatuer

amaze
amaese

amazing
amaesend

amazement
amaesness

ambassador
errend, boedberrder

amber
berrnstoen

ambiguous
twiemienend, twiesensig

ambiguity
twiemiening twiesensing

ambition
oergried, hyriech

ambitious

oergriedig,
hyriechend

ambulance
sicklingcaar, sicklingaatow, woewcaar

ambulatory
waakbaar

ambush
(v) waylaye, belaye (n) waylay, belaying

ameliorate
ferbettere

amelioration

ferbettring

amen

soew bie it, bie it soew, amen

amenable
swaybaar, miekish

amend
ferbettere, beryte, ferandere

amendment
ferandring

America
Amerrica

American
Amerriker

amiable
frendlig

amiability
frendligness

amidst
amidst

amiss

amiss

among
amung

amorous
ferluevig, luevbent
sexlustig

amount
bedraag

amount to
beluepe, (total) cueme tue, bie die saem as,
ievene out as (or at)

ampersand
entoeken, enmaark

amphibian
landwaaterdier

amphibious
landwaaterlig

ample
enuff, mennig

amplify
bestrengte, strengtene,
ferloude, ferstrange

amplifier
bestrengter, ferstranger

amplification
bestrengtness, fer-
loudness

an
yn

amuse
fermaeke, underhalte

amusing
fermaeklig, underhaltend, funnig

amusement
fermaek, tydferdrift, underhalting

anemia
bluedaarmness

anemic
bluedaarm

analogous
ferlykend, analoegish

analogy
ferlyking, analoegie

analogical
ferlykend, analoegish

analyse
untangele, unraavele, unberiddele, besundere, terrliese

analysis
untangling, unraavling, unberiddling, besundring, terrliesing

ancestor
foerfaader, ___s foer-elders

ancestral
foerfaaderlig

ancestry
offstem, foerelderlyn

anchor
anker

ancient
(adj) bissen (or soer) oeld
die ___s die classiker

and
en

anesthesia
fernumming, unfieling, unawerrness

anesthetlc
(adj) fernummend (n) fernummend middel

anesthetize
fernumme

anew
anuew, agen

angel
engel

anger
anger, torn, grammer

angry
angrig, tornig, gram

angle
winkel

Anglican
(adj) Inglish, Anglicaanish (n. -ecc.)
Anglicaaner

anguish
soelpaen, soelsmaart

angular
winklish

animal
dier

animate
belivve

animation
belivving, animaassen, trickfilm

animosity
fiendship, unfrendligness, foewship

ankle
ankel

annex
befaste, hueke aan

annexation
befasting, aanhueking

anniversary
yierday

annoint
salbe, ferhoelige

annointing
(n) salbing, ferhoeliging

annointment
salb

announce
boede, anonsse, saye out

announcement
boed, anonssing, outsaying

annoy
baadere, plaege, angere, fertorne

annoying
(adj) baadersum, plaegend, fertornend

annual
(adj) yierlig (n) yierbuek

anonymity
unbekenness

anonymous
unbekent, unnoewn

another
ynander, yn twied

answer
(v) ansere, (n) anser

answerable
feranserlig

ant
myer

antagonize
befiende, befoewe, unbefrende

antagonism
befiendship, befoew-ship, unbefrendship, wid-, taegenstand

antagonist
wid-, taegenstander

antarctic
soutpoel

antecedent
(gram) (n) foernaem, (adj) foertydlig

antedate
foertyde

ante meridiem
See a.m.

antenna
antenna

anthem
anteffen

(National) Anthem
Landssang

(Church) Anthem
him, loffsang

anthill
myerhill

anthropology
antropoloegie

anthropologist
antropoloeg, antropoloegist

anti-
wid-,taegen-

anticipate
foersie, foer- waynyme, foer-waache

anticipation
foersyt, foerwaynym, foerwaach

anticipatory
foerwaachend, foerwaynymend

antidote
widfergift, taegenfergift

antique
(adj) antiek (n) antiek

antiquities
antieklings, oeldlings

antiquated
ferantiekt, oever-oeld

antiseptic
(adj) antiseptish, widinfecsnish, taegenseptish (n) antiseptish middel, wid- ,taegeninfecsen

anvil
anvil

anxiety
unruew, wurig- ness

anxious
wurig, unruewig, begierig, yfrig

any
ennig, suem

anyone(-body)
ennigyn, huewevver

anytime
ennigtyd

apart
asunder

apartheid
asunderness, apaartness

apartment
woening, flat,
aboedling

apathy
unkerring, unkerringness, loew feeling

ape
aep

aperture
oepning, hoel

apiece
(tue, for) iech

apologetic
unshuldigend, ungiltigend

apologize
unshuldige self,
ungiltige self

apology
unshuldiging,
ungiltiging

apostle
apostel. cristfoelger,
cristfrend

apostolic
apostollish

apostrophe
apostroef, wurdmark

appall
shaake

appalling
shaakend

apparatus
aparaat

apparent
siemlig, shynlig

apparently
siembaar, shynbaar

appeal
(n) lyking, draawing, help, call

appeal to
(v) calle aan, aske for help av bie tue die lyking
av

appear
shoewe (up) (at), etie, fershyne (at)

appearance
shoewing, etieing, fershynen, foer-cuemen

appetite
ietlust, fuedcraeving, lust

appetizing
ietlustig, fuedcravend

applaud
handbyfalle, handloffe

applause
handbyfalling, handloff

apple
appel

appletree
appeltrie

appliance
houshoeldtuel, foerryting, helpmiddel

applicable
tuepasslig, tuepassbaar

applicant

tuepasser

application
tuepassing

apply
passe tue

appoint
benaeme

appointee
benaemd

appointment
benaeming

appraisal
bediemness, bedieming

appraise
bedieme

appreciate
bie tankful for, wurdige, understande,
ferstande

appreciaton
tankfulness, wurdiging

appreciative
tankful, wurdigend

apprehend
begrype, behefte

apprehension
begrip, beheft, wurrie

apprehensive
yfrig, begierig,
wurried

apprentice
lerrnling, underwurker

apprenticeship
lerrntyd, lerrntydship

approach
(v) niere, ferniere, cueme nier, cueme foerway,
genieletche, besyge (n) ferniering, genieletch

approachable
fernierbaar

appropriate
(v) geckene, beoewne, taeke for yns oewn (adj)
gedaffenlig, fit, fittend, miet, passend

appropriation
besetting, geldbesett- ing

approval
byfall, taeving

approve
taeve, billige

approximate
(v) cueme nier, falle nier, ferniere (adj) nier

approximation
ferniering

apricot
apricoes

April
April

apt
fittend, gedaffenlig, miet, passend, lyklig,
___bent, treffend

aptitude
bent (for), becwamness, fermayenness, liening
(for)

arbitrariness
wimligness,grilligness

arbitrary
oewnmaekig, grillig, oewnmytig, wimlig

arbitrate
settele, unshyde

arbitration
settling, unshyding

arbitrator
settler, shydsryter

arch
boew, (prefix) hy-

archbishop
hybisshup, hyoever- priest

archeologist
aarkioloeg(ist), oeldlyfwayscrafter

archeology
aarkioloegie oeldlyfwayscraft

architect
aarkitect

architecture
aarkitectur

arctic
nortpoel

ardent
yfrig, haat

ardour
yver, inbridness

are
due bie

Argentina
(die) Aargentin

(an) Argentine
Aargentinner

argue
beflitte, stryte,
wurdfyte, fyte
mid wurds, unynstemme,
unbestemme

argument
beflit, stryt, wurdfyt

argumentation
beflitting, stryting

argumentative
beflitbent, stryt-
bent

arise
aryse, ryse up,
stande up

aristocracy
aristocraatie

aristocrat
aristocraat

aristocratic
aristocraatish

arithmetic
reckning

arm
(n) aarm, weppen (v) beweppene, givve
weppens tue

armament
weppens, weppenwurks, beweppning

arm chair
aarmstuel, lienstuel

armistice
weppenstandstill, fythalt

armory
weppenwerrhous

armpit
aarmhoel, axel

army
hier

aroma
duft, aroema

aromatic
duftig, aroematish

around
(adv) imber, (prefix) im-

arouse
waeke, waeke up, sturre, besturre

arousal
waeking, sturring

arrange
raegele, foerordere, foersette

arrangement
raegling, foerordring, foersetting

arrest
(v) aresterre, taeke(nyme) in haft(bewerring)

(n) arest,
hafttaeking, haftnyming

arrival
hiddercueming, hidder cuemst, tuecueming,
aancuemst arrive aancueme, hiddercueme

arrogance
oeverpryd, oeverhyd, oevermied

arrogant
oeverhydish (e.g. die oeverhydish Dutchland-
ers), oeverwienend

arrow
aarow, floen, pyl

arsenal
weppenwerrhous

art
cunst

artery
ieder, slayieder, bluedberrder

arterial
iedrig, slayiedrig

article
aartikel (gram.)

articulate
(v) floewspieke (adj) floewspiekend

articulation
floewspiech

as
as, lyk, wen, **as soon as**= as suen as

ascend
goewe up, clyme, ryse, cueme up

ascendancy
upstigness, upgang, rys(ing)

ascension
See ascendancy

Ascension Day
Hevvenferrtsday, Himmelferrtsday,

ascent
beclyming, styging

aspen
aspen

aspirin
aspirin

ass
ass

assassin
(politisoh) murderder

assassinate
fermurdere

assassination
(politish) murder

assault
(n) bestorming (v) bestorme, storme

assemble
(vt) putte tuegedder, bringe tuegedder,
begaadere, betiede,

fersaamele
(vi) cueme tuegedder, gaadere

assemblage
gaadringfoelk,saamling- foelk

assembly
gaddring, saamling,

assent
ynmindness, instemming, **to assent to**- temme
tue

assert (that)
bewerre, **to assert oneself**- beryte self

assertion
bewerring

assertive
stellig, selfawerr

assess
fastsette, taxerre, feraanlaye, shatte

assessable
belastbaar

assessment
fastsetting, feraanlaying, shatting

assessor
shatter

asset
besit, foerdiel, **assets (econ.)**- activa, besittings

assign
wyse tue, bestemme

assignment
tuewysing, (school)- classwurk, hoem- wurk

assist
helpe, fultumme, stande by

assistance
help, bystand

assistant
helper, fultummer

associate
(v) ferynige, ferbinde, **to associate with**-
goewe im mid, goewe(runne) mid (n)
felloewwurker, frend

association
feryning, getieding

assonance
assonans

assume
ferunderstelle, nyme aan, understelle

assumption
aannyming, ferunder- stelling, understelling
Assumption of BVM- Hevvenwayferr

assurance
ferseckring, seckerness

assure
ferseckere

asthma
asma

astonish
oeverrashe, amaese, ferwuendere

astonishing
amaesend,oeverrashend. ferwuendrend

astonishment
oeverrashing, amaesness, ferwuendring

astound
astunde, amaese, bewildere

astounding
astundend, amaesend, bewildrend

astray
ferwaanderd, offled, offway, **to go astray**-
ferwaandere, **to be led astray**- tue bie led offway

astrologer
astroleg(er), staarfoer-teller

astrology
astroloegie, staar- foertelling

astronaut
spaasferrder, staar- ferrder, astronaat

astronomer
staarcrafter, astronoem

astronomy
staarcraft, astronoemie

astute
bryt, (hed-) smaart, intelligent, shaarp, kien

asunder
asunder

asylum
mindsicklinghous

at
at,**at first**- at furst, **at once**-
at yns, straetaway, fortwid

at present
-nouwadays, nouwig, nouwtyd

atheism
unbelief, ungaadliness, gaadbestryt, atiesem

atheist
unbeliever, gaadbestryter, atieser, frietinker

athlete
(gaem) player, sporter, atliet

athletic
sportish, atlietish

athleticism
gaemskill, sportskill

athletics
gaems, sports, atlietics

atmosphere
atmosfier, luftimerrt

atmospheric
atmosfierish

atom
atom

atomic
atommish

atone
atyne, maeke up for

atonement
atyning

atrocious
gruesum, grislig

atrocity
gruesumness, grislig died

attach
befastige, hueke, linke

attachment
befastiging, huekling, link

attack
(v) falle aan, stryke,
aete. angryfe (n) aanfall, aet

attacker
aanfaller, stryker

attempt
(v) fersieke (n) fersieking

attend
besieke,bediene **attend to**- givve hied tue,
begyme

attendance
besiekerreckning,
atwessness,
besiekertelling

attendant
besieker, bediener

attention
hied, upmaarksumness

attentive
hiedish, upmaarksum

attic
taapruem, hyruem,
underruef

attitude
mindset, mindhoeld,
stelling, hoelding

attorney
= **lawyer**

attract
pulle(draawe) foerway, draawe

attraction
draaw

attractive
draawend, handsum, luevlig, prettig, shien

attribute
(n) oewnership (v) fertrouwe tue

auction
(v) selle av, fercuepe (n) selloff, fercuep

audible
hierbaar

audibility
hierbaarness

audience
hierders, lissners, watchers, sieyers

audit
(n) geroed, buekcheck (v) duewe(maeke) buek- check

August
Aagust

aunt
taant, faadersister, muedersister, onkelfrouw

Austria
Estenryk

Austrian
Estenryker

authentic
ect, truetwurdig, atentish

authenticate
ferecte, atentikerre

author
wryter, writsteller, aator

authorship
wrytership, aatorship

authority
fullmyt, weld

authorize
mytige, ferwelde, givve fullmyt(weld) tue

auto
caar, aatow

autobiography
selflyfwryting, selflyftael

automatic
(adj) selfwurkend, (weapon) selfloedend, atomaatish (n) selfloeder(weapon)

automation
selfwurk, atomaassen., mashienwurk

autumn
fall, falltyd, haarvest

autumnal
falltydig, haarvesttydig

auxiliary
(adj) helpend (n) helper help-(helpfrouwen)

avail
diege , bediene, nuetse, helpe, **without avail-** fruetless(lig)

availability
beshickbaarness

available
frie (to be seen , used. etc). beshickbaar, foerhanden,- **suffix**- baar (cuepbaar fetchbaar)

avalanche
snoewslyd, snoewflued

avarice
gytsing, gried

avaricious
gierig, griedig

avenge
gette ieven mid, ferievene, wracke

avenging
ferievnend, wrackful

avenue
broedstriet, graetstriet, wydstriet

average
(n) middel (v) bedraage die middel, bemiddel, finde die middel

aviation
luftaart,flycraft, flying

aviator
flyer

avid
gierig, begiert, passeniert

avoid
fermyde, shunne, ferboewe

avoidance
fermyding, ferboewing

awake
(adj) awaek, awerr (v) awaeke, waeke up

award
(n) beloening, aword (v) akenne, awaarde, givve yn beloening (aword) tue

aware
awerr, awaek, **to be aware**- witte, bie awerr

away
away

awe
aaw, unsaaw, wuender

awesome
aawsum

awestruck
aawstruck

awful
aawful

awhile
awyl

awkward
aakwerd. unhandig, linkish, clumsig

awkwardness
aakwerdness, unhandigness, clumsigness

awning
windowtentling, tentling

awry
ary, amiss

axe
ax

axis
axis

axle
axel

azure
skybluew

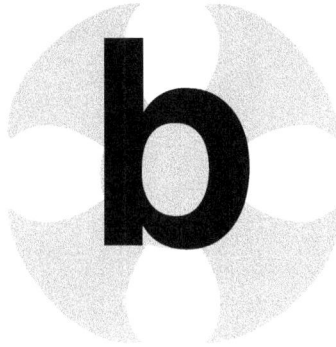

baby
litling, nuewborn, baebie

babyish
litlingish, childish

bachelor
(unmarried man) - friegesell, friefellow, (acad.)
baccalor

back
(anat.) back, ruck (return) back, eft, **back up-**
backe up, support) backe

back bone
backboen

backer
backer

backfire
(v) backfyere, fruewburste (n) backfyer,
fruewburst

background
backgrund

backing
backing

bacon

speck,
baeken

bad
baad, slet, ievil

badly
baadlig, slet

badness
baadness, ievil

badge
badg, toeken

bag
sack, poek

baggage
gepeck **baggage car**- gepeckcaar

bait
(n) baet (v) baete

bake
baeke

baker
baeker

bakery

baekrie,
baekhous

balance
(v) ferievene (n) ferievning, ievenwict

balcony
balcoen

bald
bald, herrless, call

ball
ball, cuggel

ballet
balet, balay

balloon
baluen

ballot
stemlist, hymwall

Baltic
Baltish

Baltic Sea
Esternsie

bamboo
bambuew

banana
banaan

ban
(v)ferbidde

(n)
ferbidding

band
(ring) band (mus.) muesicgruep, orkester
(group) gruep, truep (v)bande

bandage
ferband

bandmaster
muesicmaster,

muesiclieder

banish
ferbanne

banishment
ferbanning

bank
(river) uever (fin.)bank

banker
banker,geldhandler

banking
banking

bank note
banknoet

bankrupt
bankruet

bankruptcy
bankruetship

banner
banner

banquet
fest, simbel, festmiel

baptism
toep, fulwit

baptismal
toepig- **baptismal font**- toepfont

Baptist
Toeper

baptize
toepe

bar
(tavern) drinkhous, beerhous, bierhall (juris .)
laawderhued, laawship (lever) raad (v) hindere,
fersperre

barbarian
wilder, baarbaar

barbaric
baarbaarish

barbarism
baarbaarness

barber
baarber,
herrenfrisuer

bare
(adj)berr, ydel, naeked (v)ferberre, shoewe

barefoot
berrfut

barely
berrlig

barren
berren

bargain
guedcuep

bark
(n)(tree) baark (dog) baark

(v)baarke

barley
gerrst

barn
baarn, dierhous, diershelter

barometer
baromieter, baroemeter

barracks
caserrn

barrel
ton, (of a weppon)-loep

bartender
baarkiep(er)

barter
(v) ryle, toushe (n) ryl, toush

base
grundlay, fuet, baadem, bassis, grundweurk, fruemer (sports)-bass

baseball
bassball

basement
keller, underruem

basic
grundlayend, bassish

basics
grundlayings, furstlings, furstleurnings

basin
becken

basis
grundlay, baasis

bask
baske

basket
basket, corb

basketball
basketball, huepball

bass
bass

bastard
(n) underborn, unfaaderling, (adj) basterd

bat
(zoo.) bat, flyermous (sports) bat (v)batte

bath
bat

bathe
baede

bathing suit
swimclaading, swimshorts

bathroom
batruem, battimmer

battle
(n) kemp, slaag, goermitting, goud, hild, setch, fyt (v) fyt, duewe kemp

battle standard
touf, kempflag

bawl
wiepe, wyne

bay
(n) inlet,errker, bildingwing (adj) redbroun (v) baarke

be
bie, due bie (am,is,are), did bie (was, were)

beach
biech, strand

beacon
bieken, siemaark, sielyt

bead
bied

beak
biek, neb, bill

beam
biem

bean
bien

bear
(zool.) berr (v) berre

bearer
berrder

beard
bierd, wangherr, chiekherr

bearing
(mech) berring (demeanor) berring

beat
(hit) biete, hitte, slaage, gemettige (defeat) winne oever

beautician
shienmaeker, cosmettiker

beautification
fershienness

beautiful
shien, cuemlig

beautify
maeke shiener, fershiene

beauty
shienness, cuemligness

because
fordat, for, ty, forden, forwan

become
becueme

becoming
becuemend, passend

bed
bed

bed clothes
bedclaadings, sliep-claadings

bedding
bedding

bedroom
bedruem, slieptimmer

bedew
beduewe

bee
bie

beehive
biehyv, biewurks

beech
(bot) biech

beef
bief, kynflesh

beer
bier

beet
biet

beetle

bietel

before
befoer, foer

beg
begge

beggar
begger

begin
beginne, staarte

beginning
beginning, staart, fruemer

behalf
behaaf

behave
behaeve (self), bedragge (self)

behavior
behaever, bedraagen

behead
behedde

behest
behest

behind
behind,(in) back av

behold
behoelde, sie at

beholden
behoelden

behoof
behuef

behoove
behueve

being
bieing, wyt

belated
belaeted, ferlaet

belay
belaye

belch
belch

Belgian
(adj) Belgish (n) Belger

beleaguer
beliegere

Belgium
Belgerland

belief
belief, trouw

believe
believe, trouwe

belittle
belittele, ferclynere

belly
maaw, bouk

belong (to)
belange (tue), behiere (tue)

beloved
(n. pl.) belueved(-vid), lief (adj)belueved, beluevd

bell
bell

bellboy
bellyungen, bellhaap

below
beloew, dounsterrs

belt
belt

bemoan
bemoene, beclaage

bench
bench

bend
(v) bende, byge, gebigge **bend down**- bende doun, stuepe, behilde (n) bend

beneath
beniet, beloew, under, nieder

benediction
blessing, blietsing

benefactor
guedduewer, well-duewer, fremduewer

beneficial
befremmig, well-duewend

benefit
(n) frem, behuef (v) befremme

benevolence
wellwillendness

benevolent
wellwillend

benighted
benyted

benign
frendlig, kind

bent
bent

benzine
bensien

bequeath
becwiete

bequest
becwest

berate
beraete

bereave
berieve

bereft of
bereft av

berry

berrie,
berr

berth
berrt

beseech
besieche, begge

beset
besette

besetting
besettend

beside(s)
besyd(s)

besiege
besette, imselle, imsitte, imgoewe

besmear
besmiere

bespatter
bespattere

bestir
besteure

bestow
bestoewe, begivve

bestowal
bestoewing, begift

best
(adj, n) best (v) beste

bestead
bestelod

bet
(v) bewette (n) wet

betake
betaeke

bethink
betinke

betide
betyde

betimes
betyds, furstlyt

betoken
betoekene

betray
ferraade, geswyke,
bewraye

betrayal
ferraad, geswyking

betroth
betroete, ferloeve

betrothal
betroeting, ferloeft

better

better

between
betwien, in die middel(midst) av

beverage
drink

bewail
bewaele

beware
bewerre

bewilder
bewildere

bewildered
bewilderd

bewildering
bewildrend

bewilderment
bewildring

beyond
beyaand

bewitch
bewitche

bias
foerdieming, foeroerdiel

biased
foerdiemingful, bent

Bible
Bybel

biblical
byblish

bibliography
bibliograaf

bicker
bickere

bicycle
twiewieler

bid
(v) bidde (n) bid

bidder
bidder

bidding
bidding

bier
(ded) berr, lykberr

big
graet, stuer

bigamy
twiefrouwness, twieherrness, biggamie

bilabial
twielippig

bilateral
twiesydig

bilingual
twietallig, twiespiekig, twietungd

bill
(amount owed) reckning (law)bill (com) bill
(bird)bill, biek, neb (v)sende reckning

billiards
bilyerds

billion
bilyen

bind
(v) binde (n)binding (adj)bindend

binoculars
feldglasses. feldstecker, faarstecker

biography
lyftael, lyfwryting, biograafie

biographer
lieftaelwryter, biograaf

biographical
lyftaelish, biograafish

biological
bioloegish

biologist
bioloeg(ist)

biology
bioloegie

birch
burch

bird
foegel, burd

birth
burt

birthday
burtday

birthmark
burtmark

birthplace
burtsted

biscuit
cwickbred, bisk

bishop
bisshup, shyeroeversieyer

bishopric

bisdum,
oeversieyershyer

bit
(mech) bit (amount) bit, littling

bitch
(n) bitch, shiehund (v)bitche, claagge, wyne

bite
(n) byt (v). byte

biting cold
bytend coeld

bitter
bitter, gieker

bitterness
bitterness

black
(adj) black, swaartig (n)black, swaart

blackberry
blackberr(ie)

blackbird
blackfoegel, blackburd

blackboard
blackbord,chaakbord

blackmail
(n) blackmael, errpressing (v) blackmaele, errpresse

blackmarket
blackmarket

blacksmith
blacksmit

bladder
blaader, blaas

blade
blaed, halm

blame
(n) shuld, gilt, blaem, foerduemness, lie (v) begilte, foerdueme, beshulde, blaeme

bland
mild, suedend, dull

blank
blank, unbewrit, wyt

blanket
decken

blaspheme
swerre, gaadlastere

blasphemer
swerrder, gaadlasterder

blasphemous
swerrish, swerrig, gaadlastrig

blasphemy
swerring, gaadlastring

blast
(n) blast, windstoet (v) blaste (v) blaste av

blaze
(n) blaes (v) blaese

blazer
sportjacket, blaeser

bleach
(n) bliech (v) blieche

bleak
bliek

bleed
bliede

blemish
(n) flaaw, shortcueming (v) marre,beflaawe

blend
(n) blend (v) blende, gemenge

blender
blender

blending
blend, blending

bless
blesse

blessing
blessing, blietsing

blight
(n) blyt (v) blyte, widdere

blind
(n) blind, shaed, hyder (adj) blind (v)blinde, ferblinde

blindness
blindness

blink
(n) blink (v) blinke

bliss
bliss

blister
(n) blister (v) blistere

blizzard
snoewstorm

block
(n) blaak (v) blaake

blood
blued

bloodless
bluedless

bloodletting
bluedletting

blood poisoning
bluedfergift

blood pressure
blueddruck

bloodshed
bluedshed

blood vessel
bluedfet

bloody
bluedig

bloom
(n)bluem, blossem (v)blueme, blosseme

blot
(ink) clex, fleck

blot out
stryke out, wype out

blotter
clexpapier

blouse
blous

blow
(n) bloew, slaag, hit (v) bloewe

blue
bluew

blues
bluews

bluff
(n)bluff (v) bluffe

blunder
(n) blunder (v) blundere

blunt
(adj) blunt, straet, straetforway (v) blunte

blur
(n) blur (v) blurre

boar
boer

board
(n) bord (v) borde (up)

boarder
border

boarding house
bordinghous, pensioen

boast
(n) boest, roem (iv) boeste, rieme, pralle, gilpe
(trv) beroeme self, beloffe self

boastful
boestful, riemig

boat
boet

body
(gen'l) baadig, lycaam, (corpse) lyk

body guard
lycaamgaard, lyfwaacher

boil
cueke, (anger) siede

boil away
fercueke

boiler
cueker(pan), stiemkettel

boiling
cuekend, siedend

boisterous
boestrig, unruewlig, loud

bold
boeld, dapper, coef,
taenlig, chien, tryst

bolt
(n) boelt (v) boelte

bomb
(n) bom (v) bomme

bond
(n) bond (v) bonde

bondage
bondship, tralldum

bonding
bonding

bone
boen

bony
boenig

bonnet
(car) hued (headware) bonnet

book
buek

bookcase
buekhoelder

booking
bueking, foerbestelling

book-keeper
buekkieper

book-keeping
buekkieping

bookseller
buekseller, buekhandler

bookstore
buekhandel

boot
buet

booth
bued

border
(n) grens, border (v) begrense, bordere

bore
(n) boer, langwyler (v)boere, ferwaele

boring
boerish, langwylig

born
born

borough
burg

borrow
borge, baarowe

borrower
borger, baarower

bosom
buesem

boss
boss

bossy
bossig

botany
botaanie, plantwitship

botanical
botaanish, plant-

botanist
botaaniker, plantwitter

both
boed, die twie

bother
(n) baader (v)baadere, belaste

bothersome
baadersum

bottle
flask

bottom
boeden, baadem

bounce
bounse

bound
(p.p.) bunt (suffix) -bunt

boundary
grens, border

bounden
bunden

boundless
bundless

bountiful
ritch in, oeverfloewend in (mid)

bouquet
buket,(var) bucay

bourn
(stream) burn

bow (1)
(n) bouw, behild (v) bouwe, behilde

bow (2)
(n) boew (v) boewe

bowel movement
stuelgang

bowels
ingewand, innerdiel

bowl
(n)boel (v) boele

bowler
boeler

box
baax, kist

boy
boy, yungster

boyhood
boyhued, yungsterhud(-tyd)

boyscout
patfinder

brace
(n) anker, fassner, ferstranger (v) ferankere, ferstrangere

bracelet
aarmband

braces
(teeth) ankers, tandhoelders

bracken
bracken

bracket
hoelder, clamp

brag
boast

Braille
die blindalfabetbrain

brain
braen, herrsens

brake
(n- all meanings) braek (v) braeke

bramble
brambel

branch
(n) lim, bouw

branch off
ferlimme

branch out
spredde (out)

brand
(n) brand, maark (v) brande, maarke

brand name
brandnaem

brand-new
brandnuew

brandy
brandie, conyac

brass
brass

bravado
bravaadow

brave
muddig, dapper, chien,
taenlig, coef

bravery
dapperness, taenligness,
chienness, coefness

brawl
(n) brall (v) bralle

brawn
muskelstrengt

brawny
musculaar

brazen
braesen

Brazil
Brasill

Brazilian
(n) Brasiller (adj)Brasillish

bread
bred

break
(n) braek (v) braeke

breakable
braekbaar

breakage
braeken

breakfast
morgenmiel, braeke-die-fast

breath
bret

breathe
briete

breathless
bretless

breed
(n) bried (v) briede

breeze
bries

breezy
briesig

brew
(n) bruew (v) bruewe

brewery
bruewrie, bruewwurks

bribe
(n) imcuep, bestecking, byoff (v) imcuepe,
bestecke, bye av

brick
brick, baekstoen

bride
bryd

bridal
brydel

bridegroom
brydgruem

bride's maid
brydsmaed

bridge
bridg, oeverway

bridle
brydel

bright
bryt, helder

brighten
brytene, brytene up, ferheldere

brilliant
shynritch, glanzend, smaart, cwickwitted

brilliance
glanz, shynritchness

brim
brim

bring
bringe

brink
brink, edg

brisk
cwick, lyvlig,fast, spiedig

Britain
=**Great Britain**

broad
braad, wyd

broadcast
braadcaste, sende out

broadminded
braadminded, frietinkend

broil
roeste, grille, braedene

broiler
roester

broker
broeker, maacler

bronze
mestling

brook
(n) bruek(stream) (v) brueke, putte up mid

broom
bruem, swieper

broth
braat

brother
brueder **brother and sister**- sibling

brother-in-law
brueder-in-laaw, swaager

brow
brouw

brown
broun

brown sugar
brounsueger

bruise
(n) brues (v) bruese

brunt
brunt

brush
(n)brush (v) brushe

brush off
(n) brushoff (v) brushe av

brush up
(n) brushup (v) brushe up

brussels sprouts
brusselcoel

brutal
kynish, brutall

brutality
kynishness, brutallness

bubble
(n) bubbel (v) bubbele

bubbly
bubblig

buck
(n) daaler,(male deer) buck (v) bucke (av)

bucket
buckling, emmer, pael

buckle (1)
(n) buckel, clasp (v) buckele, buckele doun, buckele up

buckle (2)
(v-collapse) buckele

bud
(botany) bud

budge
yelde, bewaye, haafbewaye

budget
budget

buffalo
buffalow, byssen, wiesent

bug
bug, insect

build
(n)bild (v)bilde, bouwe, getimbere

building
bilding, bouwen, foeldboeld

builder
bilder, bouwer

bulb
(elec) biern, perr (botany)twybel

bulge
(n) swelling (v) swelle (up)

bulk
bulk

bull
bull

bump
(n) bump (v) bumpe

bumper
bumper. shaakbraeker

bun
bun

bunch
bunch, bundel

bundle
bundel

bunk
(n) bunk, wallbed (v) bunke

buoy
floet

burden
(n) burden (v) burdene

bureau
buerow, contoer

bureaucracy
buerowcraatie

burglar
inbraeker, tief, nyttief

burglarize
braeke in

burglary
braek-in

burn
(n) burn, brandwuend (vt, vi) burne (vt)
ferbrande

burrow
(n) burrow, shelterhoel, grundhoel (v)
burrowe, digge yn burrow(shelterhoel,
grundhoel)

burst
(n) burst (v) burste

bus
buss, aatowbuss

bush
bush

business
bissigness, bedrift

bust
(sculp) bust

bustle
(activity) bedriffigness, bussel

busy
bissig

but
(gram) maar, but

butcher
(n) butcher, slaaterder, slayer (v) butchere,
slaatere

butchery
butcherie, slaaterhous

butter
butter, milkspred

butterfly
butterfly, flinder

button
naap

buy
(n) by, cuep, guedcuep (v) bye, cuepe by
(gram) by

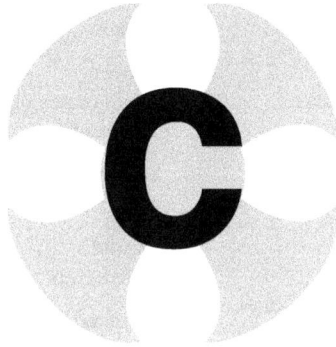

C

cab
taxie,cab, hack

cabbage
coel

cabin
cabbin,hut

cabinet
(furniture) shrank (gov't) cabinet

cabinetmaker
moebelmaeker

cable

(n)
cabbel (v) cabbele, sende yn cabbelgram

cactus
cactus

cadaver
lyk, baadig

cadaverous
lykig

cafe
coffiehous, (restaurant) cafay

cage
foeldling, penling

cake
caek

calamitous
catastroefish, woewbringend

calamity
catastroef

calcification
fercalking

calcify
fercalke

caculable
bereckenbaar

calculate
bereckene

calculating
(adj) shrued, berecknend

calculation
bereckning

calculator
bereckner

calendar
calender

calf
(zool) caaf (anat) caaf

caliber
calliber

calibrate
callibrerre

call
(n) call (e.g. It due bie yoer call.) (n-telephone) call, ruep (v-name) calle (v-shout) ruepe, calle out (v-all other meanings) calle

calligraphy
shienwryting

calling
(n) calling, beruep

calm
(adj) still,stillig, ruewig (n) stillness,
ruewigness

callous
(feeling) haardhaarted, haartless, tickfielend
(having calluses) hornig, eltig

callousness
haartlessness, tickfieling, haardhaartedness

callus
elt

calve
caave, calv

camel
camell

camera
cammera

camp
(n) camp, feldsted (v) campe, feldlaye, sette
up camp

camper
camper

campaign
(n-pol.) wallkemp, candiderring (n-mil)
feldtog (v-pol) wallkempe, candiderre (v-mil)
maeke feldtog

campaigner
veteraan, wallkemper

camphor
camfer

can
(n)can (v- able to) canne (v- preserve) canne

Canada
Caanada

Canadian
(n) Caanader (adj)Caanadish

canal
canall, waaterway

canary
canaarie

cancel
stryke out, unduewe

cancellation
strykout, undied

cancer
(med) canser, illgroewt, illswelling (astr)
Tropic of Cancer- Crabsturn

cancerous
canserish, illgroewtbefallen

candid
straetforway, trouwful

candidate
candidaat, runner

candle
candel

candle light
candellyt

candy
candie, swiets

candied
candied

cane
waakstick

cannibal
cannibal, menchfrieter

canine
(adj) hundish (n) hund

canoe
canuew

cannon
cannen

canon
canon

canonical
canonnish

canonize
hoeligfercliere

canonization
hoeligfercliering

canvas
saelcloet, saelduek

canvass
(n)sifting (v)sifte

canyon
canyen

cap
hat, muts, cap

capable
becwaam, fayig

capability
becwaamness, fayigness

capacity
(num., amt.)-inhoeld (ability)- becwaamness

capital
(money)- geld (city) - hedstad,

capital
(letter)- hedletter, **capital
crime** - capitallfoeken **capital punishment** -
detstraff

capitalize
maeke ...hedletter

hedlettere

capitalism
capitallness

capitalist
capitaller

capitulate

yelde, capitulerre,
givve up

caprice
wim, grill, loun

capricious
wimmish, grillig, lounish

capsize
(vi, vt) oeverturne, tippe oever, (vi) kentere

capsule
capsul

captain
(n) hedperson, capiten, lieder (v) capitenne,
liede

caption
(n) underwrit, hedding (v) underwryte, hedde

captor
fanger

captivate
fange, besnerre,
behefte

capivating
besnerrish, beheftish

captive
(n) fangen, heft (adj) fangen

captivity
fangenship, heftgestall, geheltsumness

capture
(n) fang, beheft (v) fange, behefte

car
caar, aatow

caramel
caramell

carbine
caarbien

carbon
coelstuff, carbon **dioxide-**
coeldioxied, **carbon monoxide-**
coelmonoxied

carbonate
caarbonaat

carbonic acid
coelsouwer

carbonize
caarbonerre, fercoele

carbonization
caarbonerring, fercoeling

carburetor
caarburaeter, fergasser

carcass
(dier)lyk, cadaaver

card
caard

cardiac
haart-

cardinal
(bird) caardinall, (rel) caardinall, (color) red

cardinal number
grundtall, grundnumber

care
(n)kerr (v) kerre

career
beruep, calling,
lyfwurk

carefree
kerrfrie, woewfrie

careful
kerrful, foersytig

carefulness

kerrfulness, foersytigness

caring
kerring

careless
kerrless

caretaker
kerrtaeker, upkieper

caress
(n) softstroek, straeling (v) softstroeke, straele
carnal- fleshlustig

carnation
caarnaassen

carnival
caarnivall, simbel

carnivore
fleshfrieter

carnivorous
fleshfrietend

carol
(n) Yuelsang (v) Yuelsinge

carp
caarp

carpenter
timmerman, wuedwurker

carpentry
timmerwurk

carpet
caarpet

carpeting
caarpeting

carrier
berrder

carrion
lykflesh

carrot
caroet

carry
berre, waye

cart
caart, waagen

carton
caarten, caardbordbaax

cartoon
caartuen

cartridge
patroen, (weapon)-
caartridg

carve

caarve

carving
caarving

cascade
waaterfall

case (1)
(container)-baax, hoelder, kist,chest,

(2)
(example, instance,patient)
byspiel, (actual state of
affairs)-byspiel (grammar) - wurdform

cash
reddig geld, handgeld

cashier
cashier

casing
wrapping

cask
drum

casket
dedkist, lykkist

cast
(n) cast (v) caste, troewe, werrpe

caste
cast

casting
casting

castle
slot

cast off
(adj) castoff (n) castoff

castrate
gelde, castrerre

casual
tuefallig, slyt, kerrless,
unformish, unplant

casuality
unfall, (mil)-kemperloss

casualness
unformishness, luesness

cat
cat

catalog(ue)
(n) cataloeg (v) cataloegiserre

catastrophe
catastroef

catastrophical
catastroefish

catch
(n)fang, (sports) ketch (v)fange,(sports) ketche

catcher
fanger,(sports) ketcher

categorical
categorrish

category
categorrie

catepillar
roup

cathedral
catedrall, hedkierk

catholic

(n)
catoeliker, (rel) Catoliek (adj) catoelish

Catholicism
Catoelishness

cattle
kyn, nieten

cauliflower
bluemcoel

cause
(n) oersack, grunds, towierd, fruem (v)
feroersacke, maeke + infinitive

caustic

bytend, shaarp,

kien

caution

(n) foersytigness,

kerr

(v) givve foersytigness

cautious
foersytig, kerrful,
werrig

cave
haalow, grundhoel

cave-in

(n)fall-in

cave in
(v)falle in, givve way

cavity
haalow, tandhoel

cease
staape, halte, blinne, hoelde up, put aan
staap tue

ceiling
ruemtaap, soeldring

celebrate
fiere

celebrated
beruemt,
bekent

celebration
fiering

celebrity
beruemtness, (person)
beruemter

celery
sellerie

celestial
hevvenlig, himmlig

celibacy
wedlessness, unweddedness

celibate
(adj) unwed(ed)

(n) unwedder

cell
(biol) sell (prison) fengness, hefthoeld

cellar
keller, underruem, clief

cellophane
sellofaan

cellular
sell-, sellulaar

celluloid
selluloid

cement
(n) sement (v) semente

cemetery
graevyaard, kierkyaard

censure
(n) untaeving, blaeme, tiening . (v) untaeve, blaeme, tiene

cent
hundred, **percent** - byhundred

centennial
hundredyierfest

center
middel, midsted, midpunt, senter

central
middel, sentrall

century
yierhundred

cereal
sereall, morgenfued, cornfued, graenfued

cerebellum
small braen (herrsen)

cerebral
braen-, herrsen-

cerebrum
graet braen(herrsen)

ceremonial
serremoenish, formish

ceremony
serremoenie

certain
secker, gewiss

certainly
secker, gewiss

certainty
seckerness

certify
betrouwe, beshynige

certification
betrouwness

certificate
betrouwing(writ), beshyniging, sertieficaat

chaff
chaff

chain
fetter, ketting, fessel

chair
stuel

chalice
kelk, wyncup

chalk
cryt

challenge
(n) outdaying, outfordring (v) daye out, fordere out

challenger
outdayer

challenging
outdayend, outfordrend

chamber
chamber

champagne
shampaan

champion
(n) (competiton)-winner, shelder, forspieker
(v) shelde, spieke for

championship
bestship

chance
(n) tuefall- **by chance**- tuefallig (v) taeke yn
tuefall

chancellor
chansler

change
(n) (difference)- ferandring (money back, loose
change)- smallgeld, backgeld (v) ferandere

channel
channel

chaos
unorder, orderlack

chapel
capell

chaplain
capellpriest, caplaan

chapter
hedding, capitell

character
caracter, roel, gued naem

characteristic
caracteristish

characterization
caracterisaassen

characterize
caracteriserre, fercaractere

charcoal
wuedcoel

charge
(n) (mil)-aanfall, (law) - beshuldiging,
aanclaag (com) - cost, (load)- laeding (v)
(mil) - falle aan (law)- beshuldige, aanclaage
(com) bereckene, **be in charge of**- be anserlig
for, havve anserliging for **take charge of**-
taeke(nyme) anserliging(liedership) av

charitable
wellferrig

charity
wellferr

chart
chaart

charter
chaarter

chase
(n) ferfoelging (v) ferfoelge. runne (goewe)
after, aete

chasm
cleft, nuwellness

chassis
understell

chaste
clien

chastity
clienness

chauffer
dryver, shoefer

cheap
chiep, billig

cheapen
chiepene

cheat
(n)chiet(er), bedrigger (v)chiete,bedrigge

cheater
chieter, bedrigger

check
(n) check, reckning (v) checke

checkbook
checkbuek

check in
(n) check-in (v) checke in

check off
checke av

check out
(n) checkout (v) checke out

checkroom
coetruem, gaardroeb

cheek
chiek, wang

cheetah
chieta

cheese
chies

chef
cuek, hedcuek, sheff

chemical
(n) kiemicall (adj) kiemish

chemist
kiemiker, apotieker

chemistry
kiemie, kiemicraft

chemotherapy
kiemoterrapie

cherish
hoelde dier, fostere, clinge tue

cherry
cherrie

chestnut
(edible nut) chestnut, castaan (color) redbroun

chest
chest, brest

chew
(n) chuew (v) chuewe

chicken
chicken

chide
chyde

chief
(adj)maen,hyest, hed- (n) boss, lieder, oeverster, hedman

chiefly
maenlig

child
child, kind, berrn, yungen

chill
(n) chill (v) chille

chilly
chillig

chime
chym

chimney
smoekpyp

chin
chin

china
errtenwerr, porselen

China
Chiena

Chinese
(adj) Chienies (n) Chienies

chip
chip

chisel
(n) bytel (v) bytele

chivalrous
ridderlig

chivalry
riddership

chloric
cloerish

chloride
cloerid

chlorine
cloer

chloroform
(n)cloeroform (v) cloeroformerre

chlorophyll
cloerofil, liefgrien

chocolate
chocolaat

choice
chuesing, pick

choir
coer

choirboy
coeryungen

choke
choeke, fersticke

choose
chuese, picke

chorus
coer

chore
choer, smallwurk

Christ
Crist

christen
toepe

Christian
(n) Cristen, Cristfoelger (adj) Cristen
Christian name- foernaem

Christianity
Cristendum, Cristenhued, Cristenness

Christianize
becristene

Christmas
Yuel, Yueltyd (rel) Cristburt

Christmas Eve
Yueltydiev

chronic
often, fieltydig

chronological
cronoloegish, tydorder-

chronology
cronoloegie tydreckning

chuckle
(n) chuckel, underlaff (v) chuckele, underlaffe

church
kierk, Gaadhous, gebedhous, (institution) Kierk

cider
appelwyn

cigar
sigaar

cigaret(te)
sigaret, sigaarling

cinder
slaag

cinema
film,shoew, filmhous

circa
arund, about

circle
(n) sierkel, ring, runder, crys (v) sierkele, loepe im

circuit
crysloep, striemcrys, rundress, imgang, **short-circuit**- crysloepbraek, imway, wydloep

circuitous
imwayend, wydloepend

circular
sierkelformish, ringformish, crysformish

circulate
sierkulerre, loepe im

circulation
sierkulaassen, imloep

circumcision
besnyding, besnydness

circumcize
besnyde

circumference
imgang, crysimgang, imfaarness

circumscribe
imwryte, imscribe

circumscription
imwrit, imscript

circumspect
foersytig, imsytig

circumspection
foersytigness, imsytigness

circumstance
imstand

circumstantial evidence
indirect bewys

circus
siercus

cite
(law) foerlaade, (quote) aanhalle, siterre

citation
(law) foerlaading (quotaton) aanhalling, sitaassen

citizen
burger

citizenship
burgership, staatburgership

city
stad, graetstad

civic
burgerlig, stadburgerlig

civil
hofflig

civilian
unkemper, siviller

civility
hoffligness

civilization
sivilisaassen, beshaaving

civilize
siviliserre, beshaave

claim
(n) fordring (v) fordere

clam
clam

clamour
(n)uproer (v) roere up. roere up for

clamorous
uproerig

clammy
clammig

clamp
clamp

clan
clan

clannish
clannish

clap
(n)clap, handloff (v)clappe, handloffe

claret
redwyn

clarification
fercliering, upcliering **clarify**- fercliere, cliere
up

clash
(n)clash, gebreck (v) clashe

clasp
(n) clasp (v) claspe

class
(n)(grade) scuelclass, yier (subject) class, cors
(social) befoelkrung (category) class (v) classe

classic
classish

classical
classish

classification
classificaassen

classify
classiferre, ferclasse

clatter
(n) clatter (v) clattere

clause
(stipulation) claasel, bestemming (grammar)
undersetning

claw
(n) claaw (v) claawe

clay
clay

clean
(adj) clien, ryn (v) cliene, rynige

cleaner
(person/thing) cliener

cleanse
clense

clear
(adj)clier, shier, swiedel (v) cliere

clearance
upcliering

clearing
cliering

clearly
clierlig, swietlig, geshaadwyslig

clear off
(vt)cliere av (e.g. die taafel)

clear up
(vt, vi) cliere up (vt) fercliere

cleave
clieve

cleavage
clief

cleaver
cliever, hacknyf

clef
kie, sluetel

cleft
cleft

clench
(n) clench (v) clenche

clemency
kindness, mildness, genaad

clement
kind, mild, genaadig

clergy
(the ___) goestlighued

clergyman
goestliger

clerical
(rel) goestlig (office) staffer-

clerk
(n) (com) fercueper (office) papierwurker,
staffer, registraar

clever
clevver

cleverness
clevverness

clew
cluew

cliche
stael outdruck

click
(n) click (v) clicke

client
cunder, shaaper

cliff
cliff

climate
climaat

climb
(n)clym (v)clyme, stigge

clinch
(n)clinch (v) clinche

clincher
clincher

cling
clinge, hoelde aan, hange aan

clinic
cliniek

clinical
clinish

clink
(n) clink (v) clinke

clip
(n) clip (v) clippe

clipper
clipper

cloak
mantel

cloak room
coetruem, gaardroeb

clock
(n) claak, stundshoewer (v) claake, tyde

close
(adj) nier (v) shutte,besluete

close by
bissen nier, nier by

closet
claddingskieper(-hoelder)

close-up
ferniering

closure
slyting, besluet

cloth
cloet, raag, duek

clothe
cloede, beclaade

clothing
cloeding, claadings

clothes line
drylyn, dryroep

clothes pin
hoeldpin

clothes press
= closet

cloud
cloud, woelk, genip

clover
cloever

clown
cloun

clownish
clounish

club
(n) (social) club (weapon) club (v)clubbe

clue
hint, fingershoew

clump
(n) clump (v) clumpe

clumsiness
clumsigness

clumsy
clumsig

cluster
(n) cluster (v) clustere

clutch
(n) clutch, cupling, grip (v) clutche, grippe

coach
(n) (car) caar, buss (sport) coech, traener (v) coeche, traene

coal
coel

coalesce
ferynige, groewe tuegedder, fersmelte

coalescence
feryniging, fersmelting

coast
coest, sieshoer

coarse
raaw

coarseness
raawness

coat
(n) coet, mantel, oevershurt

coat
(v) belaye

coating
belaying

cobra
coebra

cobweb
caabweb, spinweb

cocain(e)
cocaen

cock
(n) (male fowl, part of firearm) caak (v) caake

cockpit
caakpit

cockroach
caakroech

cocoa
coecow

coconut
coeconut

cocoon
cocuen

cod
caad, cabbelyouw

coddle
pampere,caadele

code
(n) coed, laawbuek, hymwrit (v) putte (wryte) in coed

co-ed
gemengupfostring(g.u.f.)

coerce
twinge

coercion
twang

coercive
twingend

co-exist
livve in frid, bestande belyk

co-existence
belyk, bestand

coffee
coffie

coffee pot
coffiepot, coffiemaeker

coffin
dedkist, lykkist

cohabit
livve saamen(tuegedder)

cohabitation
saamenlivving

coherence
saamenhang

coherent
saamenhangend

coil
spirall

coin
munt

coincide
falle tuegedder, stemme oeveryn

coincidence
tuefall, oeveryn- stemming

coincident
oeverynstemmend

coincidental
tuefallig

Coke
Coek

cold
(n) (illness) fercoelding, coeld (adj)coeld

collaborate
wurke saamen(tuegedder) aarbyde
saamen(tuegedder)

collaboration
saamenwurk, saamenaarbyd

collaborator
saamenwurker, saamenaarbyder

collapse
(n) dounfall, fall (v) falle in (doun)

collar
(around neck) neckband (clothing)craag

collect
fergaadere, fersaamele

collection
fergaadring, fersaamling

colleague
fellowwurker, fellowaarbyder

college
(institution) univerrsitaet, oeverhyscuel (to go
to college)-goewe tue
oeverhyscuel, goewe tue die univerrsitaet

collide
stoete saamen(tuegedder) crashe, hitte hed-aan

collision
saamenstoet, crash, hed-aan

colonial
coloniall

colonist
colonier

colonize
coloniserre

colonization
colonisassen

colony
colonie

colloquial
imgangspieklig, gemaensum

colloquialism
gemaen

color
faarben

colorblind
faarbenblind

colorblindness
faarbenblindness

colorful
faarbenritch

colt
coelt, foel

column
(typography) spalt (pillar) piller, coloen

coma
diepsliep, mindnumnrss

comatose
diepsliepig, mindnummend

comb
(n)coem (v) coeme

combat
(n) kemp, fyt, goud (v) kempe, fyte

combatant
kemper

combative
kemplustig, fytlustig

combination
ferbinding

combine
ferbinde, menge, blende

combustible
brandbaar, burnbaar

combustion
ferbranding

come
cueme

coming
(arrival) aancumst, tuecueming

comedian
coemiker, laffmaeker, belaffer

comedienne
= **comedian**

comedy
blydsumness, funlust

comic
(n) = comedian (adj) coemish, funnig, belaffig

comical
= (adj) **comic**

comfort
(n)troest, suedness, behaagligness (v) troeste

comfortable
suedend, behaaglig

comforter
(person) troester (bed cover) cwilt

comely
cuemlig, ferr

command
(n)behest, geboed, bidding, herrship (v)bidde, beherre

commander
behester, hiertoeger, hildfruemer

commanding
(adj) indruckwaekend, graet(e.g., a commanding lead)

commando
comandow

commemorate
betinke

commemoration
betinkness

commemorative
betink-, betinkish

commence
beginne, staarte

commencement
beginning, staart, aanfang, (gradua- tion ceremony)- diploembestoewing

comment
(n) bemaarking (v) bemaarke

commentary
comentaar

commentator
melder

commerce
bissigness, handel

commercial
(n) reclaam (adj) handels-, sell-

commission
(n) ferweldhued, comissen (v) ferwelde, givve fullmyt tue, comissene

commissioner
ferwelder, comissionaar

commit
(deed) duewe, maeke, begoewe, fertrouwe, **commit oneself to**- binde self tue, **commit adultery**- braeke wedlaak

committed
selfbund(-tyd,- held) tue

commitment
selfbond

committee
ferweldhued, comitie

common
(all)gemaen, allfoelkish, bewoenlig

commonality
gemaenness, bewoenligness

commotion
uproer

communal
gemaenshiplig

commune
(n)gemaener, allfoelkferyning (v)wye(e.g. wye mid natuer) **communicable**- fortsendbaar, imsendbaar,

communicate
(vt) bewitte, benoewe (vi) betyde, stande in ferbinding mid

communication
ferbinding **communion** (rel) Housel, gemaenship

communism
communissem

communist
communist

communistic
communistish

community
(lit.) toun, burg, torp + (fig) fellowship, tuegedderness,

gesaamling
(used descriptively-adj) gemaen, allfoelkish + *Toun* and *burg* may be used as combining forms: *Tounmeeting, burgfersammling*, etc.

commute
(vt) (change) ferandere (travel back and forth)-(vi)swinge

commutation
ferandring

companion
befierder, shoelderfrend, gesell, maet

companionship
befierdership,maetship gesellship, gemoen

company
(social-fig)=**companionship** (social-visitors) besieker(s) (com) companie, handelssack (mil)

companie

comparable
ferlykbaar, lykenbaar

comparative
ferlykend

compare
(beyond, past, ___)-

unferlykbaar
(v) ferlyke, belykene

comparison
ferlyking, **in comparison with**- in ferlyking mid

compartment
offdieling, fack

compass
wayniedel, compaas

compassion
lyksaarow, lyksorg, errbaarmen

compassionate
lyksaarowful, lyksorgenful

compatibility
berrbaarness, ferynigbaarness

compatible
ferynigbaar, **compatible (consistent) with**-ferynigbaar mid

compatriot
landsman

compel
twinge

compelling
twingend

compensate
ferguede, betalle back, maeke up for, compenserre, maeke gued die ___

compensation
fergueding, unlossiging, errsaats

compete
(sports only) playe agenst, widplaye(all meanings)- wid-, taegenkempe concurerre, (com only)- sellkempe

competence
becwaamness

competent
becwaam

competition
(sports only)widplay, (all meanings)wid-
,taegenkemp,

concurens,
(com. only)- sellkemp

competitor
(sports only) widplayer, (all meanings)-wid-,
taegenkemper, concurent, (com only)-
sellkemper

competitive
(sports only) widplaybaar, (all meanings)-
wid-, taegenkempbaar, concurerrend

complacence
(self) tuefridness

complacent
(self) tuefridden, (bie) befrid mid self

complain
claage oever, yiemere

complaint
claag, yiemring, murkning

complement
(n) (grammar)- outfiller, **full complement-**
die full number

complementary
outfillend

complete
(adj) fullstandig, fullcuemen, (absolute) -
full, totall (v) fille out, fullduewe, bringe tue
yn end

completion
outfilling, endiging

completely
fullcuemen, fullen, fullstandend, fullswyd

completeness
= **completion**

complex
(adj) (difficult) haard, mutchlayerd, swyrig,
ferwickeld (n) wiev av housing, housingwiev

complexion
ansytfaarben

complexity
haardness, mutchlayerdness, ferwickling

compliance
inwilliging, inferstandness

complicate
maeke mutchlayerd, ferwickele, complikerre

complication
(all meanings) - complicaassen

complicity
midshuld, midgilt. giltsherr

compliment
(n) compliment (v) complimenterre, givve yn
compliment tue

complimentary
complimentish, frie **complimentary ticket-**
frie ticket

comply
yelde, behorke, givve in tue

component
underdiel, bestanddiel

compose
stelle saamen, putte tuegedder, **control
oneself-** bestiere self, ferstille self **compose
music-** wryte muesic, componerre muesic,
(print)-sette typ

composer
wryter, saamensteller, typsetter

composition
saamenstelling, wryting

composure
(control) selfbestiering

compound
(n) ferbinding, blending, saamensetting,
(prison)- fangnessyaard, **compound fracture-**
twiefoeld boenbraek, **compound interest-**
twiefoeld intrestbetalling, **compound
sentence-** twinsetning (v) ferblinde, blende,
sette saamen(tuegedder) (**make worse**)-
ferweurse, weursene (**increase**)- fergraetere

comprehend
understande, ferstande, begrippe, graspe

comprehensible
understandbaar, ferstandlbaar, begripbaar

comprehension
ferstandness, begrip

comprehensive
wydswiepend, allswiepend

compress
(n) saamenpresser (v) drucke saamen
compressed air- druckluft

compression
saamendrucking

compressor
saamendrucker

comprise
bie maed up av, laake in

compromise
(n) haafway- oeverynstemming,
haafwayyelding, haafwaymieting (v) yelde
haafway, miete haafway **compromise oneself**-
lieve self oepen tue, laye self oepen tue

compulsion
twang, niedbedaarfing

compulsive
twingend

compulstory
getwangen,obligatorrish, must-

computation
bereckning, raaming

compute
bereckene, raame

computer
compueter

computerize
fercompuetere

comrade
befierder, shoelderfrend

concave
concaav

conceal
hyde, ferberrge, ferhymlige

concealment
hyding, ferhymliging, ferborgenness

concede
(tr) givve up (intr) givve in, bewillige

conceit
ferbilding, selfloff

conceited
ferbilded

conceivability
tinkbaarness

conceivable
tinkbaar

conceive
becueme swanger, ferstelle tue self, ferbilde tue
self, chenne, tinke up(out)

concentrate
bemiddele yns hied (or taats), bringe saamen
(tuegedder), consentrerre

concentration
hiedbemiddling, saamenbringing,
consentraassen

concept
begrip, idie, taat

conception (pregnancy)
swangership- **Immaculate Conception**-
die Unbefleckt Swanger- ship, (idea)
foerstelling, begrip

concern
(n) (matter)-sack (bus, firm) bedrift
(emotion)- wurrig, kerr (v) havve tue duewe
mid, wurrige, betreffe

concerning
(prep) betreffend

concert
conserrt

concise
short, bondig

conciseness
shortness, bondigness

conclave
hymlig -,cardinallsitting

conclude
beslisse, endige,

conclusion
besluet, end

conclusive
beslissend

concrete
(n) beton (adj) wurklig

concur

bedwerre,
stemme oeveryn, bie av yn mind

concurrence
bedwerring , oeveryn- stemming, ynmindness

concussion
braenshaak

condemn
ferdamme, dueme

condemnable
ferdambaar

condemnation
ferdamming, duem

condemnatory
ferdammend

condense
(liquids) ferticke, tickene (gen'l)shortene, condenserre

condensation
ferticking, condensaassen

condescend
ferneddere self mid, ferievene self mid

condescending
ferniedrend, ferievend

condescension
ferniedring,

ferievning

condition
(n) tuestand, betinging, fettel, araadness, gestall, staadel, shaep **on condition that**-
aan betinging (widden) dat (v) betinge

conditional
betingd, condissionell

conditioning
shaepreddigness, ferfettling

condole
morne mid, condolerre mid

condolence
midmorning, condolenz

condom
condom, contraseptiv, swangershipfoerstaller

condone
fergivve, oeverlueke

condor
condor

conducive (tue)
beforderlig for, lienend tue

conduct
(n) behaever, bedraagen (v) liede, behaeve, bedraage

conductor
lieder, bestierder, (public conveyance)-
ferrsaammler

cone
kiegel, (ice cream)- coen

confection
suegergueds, swiets

confectionery
suegergueds, swietshous

confederacy
ferbond, the **Confederacy**- die Soudern Ferbond

confederate
bondpaartner, ferbonden, Ferbonden (av die Soudern Ferbond)

confederation
= **confederacy**

confer
(vi) taake oever, ferlende (vt) begivve, bestoewe

conference
bespieking, conferenz

confess
andette, bekenne, (hum) fesse up, (rel) bicte

confession
andet, bekenness, (rel) shrift, sintelling

confessional
bictstuel, confessionell

confessor
(one who c.) -bekenner, (rel) bicter- (one who hears c.) -bictfaader

confidant
fertrouwling

confide
(vi) (c. in s.o.) fertrouwe in (vt) (reveal)
fertrouwe (tue)

confidence
fertrouwen, selfbelief, selftrust

confident
secker, selftrustend, fertrouwen

confidential
fertrouwlig

confiding
trustful, fertrouwensful

confine
begrense, shutte in, hoelde in, ferkiepe

confines
innerings

confinement
ferkieping, -bund (e.g. housbund, bedbund,
snoewbund)

confirm
(a report, new Church members)-befastige,+ (a
belief, fear)- strengtene, (determine validity)-
becraftige+

confirmation
(of a report, new Church members)-
befastiging, (of a belief, fear, etc)-fer-
strengt, strengtning, (validity)- becraftiging+
+ *Befastige* and *becraftige* are synonymous
when *befastige* refers to a report. *Befastiging*
and *becraftiging* are synonymous in the same
sense.

confiscate
laawgraspe, laawgrippe, beslaynyme

confiscation
laawgrasp, laawgrip, beslaynym

conflagration
graet brand(fyer)

conflict
(n) fyt, struggel (v) fyte, struggele, (contradict) taegenspieke

conflicting
(stories, evidence, testimony) -fershillend,
anders, unlyk

conform
duewe lyk, faalowe, foelge, maeke oeveryncuemstig

conformity
oeverynstemming, **in conformity with**- (prep)
oeveryncuemstig

confound
bewildere, befaage, becloude, befuddele

confront
stande befoer, bringe (sette)before, miete
ansyt tue ansyt, confronterre

confrontation
foersetting, foerstand, confrontaassen

confronting
standen befoer

confuse
= confound

confusing
bewildrig

confusion
bewildership, unclierness

congenital
atburt-, av (at) burt

congest
oeverfille, claage, oevercroude

congested
oeverfild, oeverfull, claagd, oever crouded

congestion
(med) bluedhaest, oeverfullness,
oevercroudedness

congestive heart failure-
haartstryk av bluedhaestning

congratulate
wishe s.y. gued luck, wishe s.y. well, gratulerre

congratulation(s)
guedluckwish, **Congratulations!**-
Guedluckwishes!, Ick due gratulerre yue!

congregate
gaadere, saamele, cueme tuegedder

congregation
gaadring, saamling, (rel) gemient,
congregaassen, flaak

congregational
(rel) congregaassionell

congress
(body)die Laawmaeker- hued, (congressmen)-
Laawmaekers, die Laawmaekerhouses,
Congress

congressional
av die Laawmaeker- hued (die Laawmaekers,
die Laawmaekerhouses)

conic
kieglish, coenish

conifer
niedeltrie

conjecture
(n) gessing, gesswurk (v)gesse

conjugal
wedrytig, ectlig

conjugate
(gram) inflecte, belinke

conjugation
(gram) inflected forms, belinking

conjunction
(gram) ferbinding

conjunctive
ferbindend

conjure
(spirits) beswerre (ideas) tinke up

conjuration
beswerring

connect
ferbinde, belinke

connected
ferbund, belinkt

connecting
ferbindend, belinkend

connection
ferbinding, belinking,
link

conquer
(territory) feroevere, oevertroewe. bedwinge
(games, people) winne oever oeverwelme

conqueror
feroeverder, bedwinger

conquest
feroefring, bedwinging

conscience
bewitten, rytwitten

conscientious
upryt, kerrful

conscientiousness
uprytness, kerrfulness

conscious
awerr, bewust

conscript
(n) draftling (v) drafte, calle up

conscription

draft , callup

consecrate

inwyde,
ferhoelige, maeke hoelig, blesse, hallowe

conscecration
ferhoeliging, blessing, inwyding

consecutaive(ly)
ynanderfoelgend, fortloepend, in a roew

consensus
oeverynstemming

consent
(n) tuestemming, inwilliging, betaffing, liev
(v) stemme tue, inwillige, givve liev, betaffe

consequence
foelging, afterhappning

conservation
(natural res.)- natuerupkiep (gen'l)
upkiep,belasting

conserve
belaste, kiepe up

conservative
(adj) conserrvativ (n) (politics) conserrvativ

conservatory
conserrvator

consider
waye oever, tinke about(oever), besinne,

besmie, betinke

considerable
bissen, mennig

considerate
taatful, kerrend

consideration
taatfulness, kerring, oeverwaying

consignment
besending

consist of
maeke up av, bestande av (or in)

consistence
(liquids) tickness, ferynbaarness, saemness, oeverynstemming

consistency
=consistence

consistent
ferynbaar, saemnesshoeldend

consolation
troest, suedness, friever

consolable
troestbar, suedbaar

console
troeste, suede, frievere

consoling
troestend, suedend

consolidation
fersaamling, feryning, ferfastiging, ferstrangerness

consolidate
putte(bringe) togedder, fersaamele, feryne, ferfastige, ferstrange

consonant
(gram) unglyd, unclinker

conspicuous
outstandend, strykend, oeversiebaar

conspicuousness
outstandness, oeversiebaarness

conspiracy
saamenswerring, ferswerring

conspirator
saamenswerrder,

ferswerrder

conspire
swerre saamen(tuegedder) ferswerre

constant
(adj) alltydish,stedfast, unferanderlig, aangoewend, unendend (n) alltyder, unferanderder

constancy
unferanderligness, stedfastness, bestandigness

constantly
bestandig, fortwyl, iefrig, stedfast

constellation
staarsaamling, staargaadring

constipation
ferstaaping

constipate
ferstaape, staape up

constituency
stemmershyer, stemmerhued

constitute
maeke up, sette saamen (tuegedder)

constitution
maekup, saamensetting **United States Constitution**- die Constituessen av die Ferynd Staats

constitutional
laawful, laawgrunded, constituessionell

constrain
betwinge

constrained
betwingd

constraint
twang

construct
bilde, bouwe, getimbere

construction
bilding, bouwing, construcsen

constructive
upbildend, upbouwend, constructiv

construe
fercliere, laye out

consul
consul

consulate
consulaat

consult
seeke die raad av, consulterre

consultant
beraader, raadgivver

consultation
beraading

consultative
beraadend

consume
iete, drinke, ferbrueke, fernittige, geforme

consumer
ferbrueker

consumption
ferbruek

contact
(n) beruering, contact (v) maeke contact mid, putte self in ferbinding mid

contagious
aanstickend

contain
befatte, hoelde in

contamination
befouling, besmutting, durtigness

contaminate
befoule, besmutte

contemporary
(n) saemtyder (adj) saemtydig nouwtydig

contempt
ferhied, scorn, **contempt of court**- unhoffligness(scorn) for die hoef

contemptible
ferhieding

contemptuous
ferhiedlig, scornful

contend
fyte for, kempe for, **to contend that**- hoelde dat

content
(adj) tuefridden (n) inhoeld

contention
stryf, wrangel, beflit

contentment
tuefriddenness

contents
= **content**

contest
(n) strid, taegenkemp (v) bestridde, daye(fordere)out

context
saamenhang

continence
selfbestiering

continent
(adj) (moderate)- mettig (n) continent, errtdiel
the Continent- die Fastland av Euroepa

continental
continentall

continual
aangoewend, fortduerend

continuance
bestendiging

continuation
aangoewendness, fortsetting, ferfoelg

continue
(tr) goewe aan + -en inf., (iv) goewe aan + time, place expression kiepe aan + -en inf., fortsette, ferfoelge

continuity
saamenhang, unbroekenness

continuous
unbroeken, unendend, aangoewend

contraception
widtaegenswangership

contraceptive
(adj)swangershipblaakend, contraseptiv (n) swangershipblaak, contraseptiv, condom

contract
(n) oeverynstemming (writ), saamendraawing, oeveryncuemst (v) laake intue yn oeverynstemming(saamendraawing, oeveryncuemst), contracterretue

contradict
widspieke, spieke taegen, goewe agenst

contradiction
widspiech, taegenspiech

contradictory
widspiekend

contrary
(adj) widset, widdig **on the contrary-**
inwiddiel, intaegendiel

contrast
(n) widstelling, taegenstelling, contrast (v)
shoewe widstelling (fershillen)

contrasting
widstellend, taegenstellend

contribute
bydraage, givve tue

contribution
gift, bydraag, shenk

contrite
(sorgen-) saarowful, berouwful

contrition
diep saarow (sorg),berouw

contrive
tinke up (av), betinke contrived foerplant

contrivance
aparaat, betinksel

control
(n) myt, hoet, bestiering controel, helm (v)
bestiere, controele

controversial
wurdfytish, betwist, beflittend, stryt

controversy
wurdfyt, beflitt imstritten

convalesce
genaese, winne back yns helt, ferbettere

convalescence
genaesing, nuewhelt, ferbettring

convalescent
genaesend, nuewheltig **convalescent care-**
afterbehandling

convene
fersaamele, fergaadere, calle tuegedder, ruepe
saamen

convience
tydsperrder (-saever), gerissen, ferieding

convenient
feriedig, gerissenlig, ynfack

convent
sisterhous, cluester

convention
fersaamling, saamencuemst

conventional
bewoenlig, gebrueklig, convensionell

converge
cueme(strieme) tuegedder, convergerre, loepe
saamen

convergence
saamenstrieming, saamenloeping, converrgenz,
cuemingtuegedder

conversant
fertrouwd

conversation
taak, gespreck conversational sprecksum,
taaksum

converse
sprecke, spieke(taake) mid, underhoelde,
taake, converserre

conversion
gecherring, ferandring

convert
gecherre, ferandere, converterre

convertible
feranderbaar, converterrbaar, (car) taapfoelder

convey
bringe oever, befordere, bewaye, berre

conveyance
befordring, bewaying

conveyer
oeverbringer **conveyer belt-** loepend band

convict
(n) straffanger, straffling (v) finde
giltig(shuldig), bewyse(befande) giltig(shuldig)

conviction
giltfinding, shuldfinding, oevertyging

convince
oevertyge, swaye

convincing
oevertygend, swayend

convulsion
heftig muskeltwitch

cook
(n) cuek (v) cueke

cooker
cueker

cooking
cueking

cool
(adj) cuel (v)cuele (av)

coolant
fercueling

cooler
cueler

coolness
cuelness

co-operate
midwurke, wurke tuegedder(saamen)

co-operation
midwurk, saamenwurk (-aarbyd)

co-operative
(n) fersherring (adj) midwurkend

co-ordinate
(adj) lykorderd, ievenwictig (v) bringe intue
oeverynstemming, ferynige, coordinerre

co-ordination
oeverynstemming- bringing, midwurk(ing),
coordinaasen

cop
polieser

cope
ferievene mid

copper
caaper

copier
(person) lyk-, afterduewer (thing)
coperrmashien, coperrtuel

copy
(n) offwrit, copie, byspell (v) coperre, duewe
lyk (after)

copy cat
= **copier (person)**

corral
corall, imfoeld, horsfoeld

cord
(all meanings) cord, roep

cordial
(adj)haartlig, frendlig (n) swietlicoer

cork
cork

corkscrew
corkscruew

corn
corn, maes

corner
eck

coronary
(med) coronaar

coronate
becroune

coronation
becrouning

corporal
(adj) boedig, lycaamlig (n) corporall **corporal
punishment**- boedig(lycaamlig) bestraffing

corporate
corporaat

corporation
corporaassen, feryniging corporeal lycaamlig

corpse
lyk

correct
(adj) ryt, rytig, correct (v) berytige, ferbettere,
corigerre

correction
berytiging, ferbettring **House of Correction**-
gefangness

corrective
berytig, ferbettring-

correspond
stemme oeveryn, lykene tue, bewitte, corresponderre

correspondence
oeverynstemming, lykness, letterwissling, **correspondence school**- maelscuel, postscuel

correspondent
letterpaartner, beryter, melder

corresponding
ferlykend, alyk

corridor
hall, hallway, passway, waakway

corrigible
ferbetterbaar

corrode
ferruste, ruste (away), friete away

corrosion
ferrusting, wayfrieting

corrosive
(adj) bytend, infrietend (n)infrieter

corrupt
(adj) imcuepbaar,raaten (v) imcuepe, bye off, ferraate

corruptible
imcuepbaar, byoffbaar

corruptibility
imcuepbaarness

corruption
unoerligness, raatenness

corruptive
badmaekend

corsage
shoelderbluem, corsaag

corset
corset

cosmetic
(adj) cosmettish, shienness- (n) cosmettic, shiennessmiddel

cosmic
cosmish, hoelweldig

cosmography
cosmograaf

cosmonaut
(spaes-) ruemtferrder, cosmonaat

cosmos
cosmos, hoelweld

cost
(n) cost (v) coste

costly
costlig

costume
costuem, claddingset

cot
foeldbed, bedling

cottage
frietydhous, housling

cotton
boumwull

couch
couch, soefa

cougar
cueger

cough
(n)coff, huesten (v)coffe, hueste

cough syrup-
(huesten-)coffmiddel

could
cud

council
raadfersaamling

councilor
raadfersaamlinger

counsel
(n)(advice) raad (lawyer) laawwitter (v) beraade

counsellor
beraader, raadgivver

count
(n) reckning, telling (v) telle, beryme

countenance
(n) ansytluek (v) boelstere, taeve, billige

counter
teller, berymer, sydbord, taenbord **counter-balance**- offsette

counterfeit
(adj) aftermaed, fals (v)ferfalse

countermand
calle back yn order

countersign
waachwurd, passwurd

countless
untoeld, untellbaar,
unrym

country
(nation) land, hoemland, faaderland (rural)
die land, outland

countryman
(fellow)landsman

county
shyer, understaat **county seat-** shyersiet

couple
perr, twie

coupon
cuepon, prysticket

courage
muet, taenligness

courageous
muetig, dapper, taenlig

courier
runner

course
(educ) cors (gen'l) run **golf course-** golfsted **of
course-** natuerlig, selfferstandlig

court
(n) hoff, (sports) playfeld, (law)gerytshoff (v)
wuewe, goewe (out) mid

courteous
hofflig

courtesy
hoffligness

court-martial
(n) hierferhandling (-ferhiering) hierprosess **to
be court-martialed-** bie ferhierd (ferhandeld)
by gerytshoff

courtship
wuewing

cousin
(m & f) cuesin, onkelsoen, onkeldaater,
taantsoen, taantdaater

cove
coev

covenant
ferbond

cover
(n)deck, bedecking, welf (bottle, box) deckel,
lid, taap (v) bedecke, bewelve

covering
bedecking, overlay, belaying

covert
hidden, hymlig

covet
begerre, craeve

covetous
begerrig, craevend

covetousness
begerrigness, strang wilning, craeving

cow
couw

cowboy
couwherrder, couwman, herrdryder,
couwpuncher

coward
fierclinger, couwerling, craeven

cowardly
fierclingend, fierbent, craeven

cower
couwere

cowl
munkhued

coyote
kyoetie, kyoet

crab
crab

crack
(n) crack, split (v)cracke

cracker
cracker

cradle
(n)craedel (v)craedele

cradelsong
craedelsang, lullaby

craft
(n) craft, handwurk, slyness, cunning (v)crafte
--craft --craft craftsman craftsman,
handwurker crafty craftig, sly, cunning

craftiness
craftigness,slyness, cunning

cramp
cramp

crane
(zo) craan (mech) craan

crank
(n) crank (v) cranke

cranky
crankig

crash
(n) crash (v) crashe

crashland
crashlande

crate
kist, wickerwurk

crater
craater

crave
craeve,ferlange

craving
craeving, ferlangen

crawl
(n) crall (v) cralle

crawl space
crallruem

crayfish
crayfish

crayon
pastell(stick)

craze
craes

craziness
craesigness

crazy
craesig

creak
(n) criek (v) crieke

creaky
criekig

cream
(n)(edible)roem, (inedible) criem (v) roeme

cold cream-
coeldcriem

whipped cream-
wipt roem

creamy
roemig, criemig

crease
(n)foeld,wrinkel (v) foelde

create
sheppe, fremme

creation
shepping

first creation-
fruemership

creative
sheppish

creativity
sheppishness

creator
shepper, sheppend **creature**- wyt, bieing

credence
belief

credentials
beliefletter rytspapier

credibility
beliefwurdigness beliefbaarness

credible
beliefwurdig beliefbaar

credit
trust, belief

creek
criek, striem also: crick

creep
criepe

creeper
crieper

creepy
criepig, kerrig

cremate
ferbrande

cremation
lykferbranding

crematory
lykueven, lykuevenhous

Creole
Croel

crepe
craep

crescent
(adj) waxend (n)muensykel, haafmuen

cress
cress

crest
(n) (highest point)-ridg, taap (tuft) - coem (v) rieche die taap

crevice
cleft, briech

crew
bemanning, shipfoelk, luftcraftfoelk. wurkerhued

crib
crib, litlingbed

crick
(pain in neck,back)- crick (criek) crick

cricket
(insect,sport) cricket

crime
misdied, foeken, fyren, ferbraeken, laawbraeking

crime novel
criminallromaan

criminal
(adj) ferbraekish, criminall, unlaawful (n) ferbraeker, laawbraeker, criminall, outlaaw

crimson
diepred, bluedred

cringe
cringe

cripple
(n) yn crippel (v) crippele, maeke laem, gebigge

crippled
crippeld, laem

crisis
crissis, turnpunt

crisp
(adj) crisp (v)crispe

criteria, criterion-
mets, met

critic
critieker, faltfinder

critical
critish, faltfindend

criticize
critiserre, finde falt mid

criticism
critiek

crockery
errtenwerr

crocodile
croecodil

crocodile tears
croecodiltiers

croon
cruene

crooner
cruener

crop
craap

cross
(adj) mien (n) cross, rued (v) crosse, crosse oever, cueme (goewe)oever

crossbar
crossbaar

crossbreed
crossbriede

crosscheck
crosschecke

cross-country
oeverland, crossland

cross-examination
crossferhiering

cross-examine
crossferhiere

cross-eyed
crost ygen

crossing
crossing

cross-reference
(n) crossreferring (v) crossreferre

crossroad
crossroed, crossway

crosswalk
crosswaak

crossword
crosswurd **crossword puzzle-**
crosswurdraadsel

crotch
craach

crouch
(n) scwaat (v) ducke (doun), scwaate, sitte aan yns hiels

crow
(n) croew (v) croewe

crowbar
croewbaar

crowd
(n) croud, trang, gemang (v) croude

crowded
crouded, oeverfull

crown
(n) croun, hedwriet (v) becroune

crucial
crittish, wictig, beslissend

crucifix
crossifix

crucifixion
crossiging

cruciform
crossformig

crudity
raawness, ruffness

cruel(ly)
mien, rielig, unfielend, unkind

cruise
(n) genuegensieress, sieress, crossing (v) taeke yn sieress

cruiser
poliescaar

crumb
crum

crusade
(n) (rel) crusaad, hoelig oersack, fyt, oersackfyt (v)fyte, fyte for yn oersack

crush
(n) crush, underdruck, infatuaassen (v)crushe, underdrucke

crust
crust

crustacean
crayfish, crusten-

crutch
crutch

cry
(n)shout, call, outburst (v) shoute, calle, wiepe, betiere, shedde tiers

crypt
undergrundruem

cryptic
hidden, hymlig

crystal
cristall

crystaline
cristallen

crystalize
cristalliserre

cub
welp, offspring, yung

Cuba
Cueba

Cuban
(n) Cueber (adj) Cuebish

cube
cueb

cubic
cuebish

cubit
cuebit

cubicle
sliepfack,
fackling

cuckoo
cuecuew

cucumber
gurk

cud
cud **chew the cud**- chuewe die cud, tinke
oever, waye oever

cuddle
cuddele (up)

cudgel
cudgel

cue
(n) (bilyerd) cuew, hint, beminding (v)hinte,
beminde

cuff
(n) cuff (v) cuffe

cuisine
cuekway, cueking

culminate
pieke

culminating
piek, hyest

culmination
piek, hyest punt

culpability
gilt, shuld

culpable
giltig, shuldig

culprit
wrangduewer, giltiger, shuldiger

cult
wurshipway, tillergruep, foelgergruep, cult

cultivate
tille

cultivation
tilling

cultural
culturell, cultuerish

culture
cultuer, brieding, riering

cultured
cultuerd, wellbred

cumbersome
burdensum, clumsig, unweldig

cunning
(n) cunning, craft, list (adj) craftig, listig

cup
cup

cupboard
cupbord, shrank, ietwerrhoeld

curable
hielbaar

curative
behielig, ferwellig, heltbringend

curate
underpriest,

helpgoestliger

curator
behierder

curb
(n) curb(stoen), hoeldback, strietedging (v)
curbe, hoelde back, bestiere, controele

curd
curd

curdle
curdele

cure
hiele

curfew
hoemstund, tydlyn

curious
witgyrig, nuewsgyrig, wityfrig

curiosity
witgyrigness, wityfrigness

currant
crent

currency
betellmiddel, betellmiens, geld, nouwness
foreign currency- outlandgeld

current
(adj) loepend, nouwtydig, allgemaen (n)
striem, strieming, waaterpull

curriculum
corslisting, studerrplan

curse
(n) curs (v) curse, swerre

cursed
curst

cursive
(adj) loepend, runnend (n) loepend wryting

cursor
loeper, runner

curt
unhofflig, bytend

curtail
beshiere, loewere, cutte short

curtailment
beshiering

curtain
gordyn, foerhang

curtsy
(n)bouw, bend (v)bouwe, bende

curve
(n)bend, (baseball)- bender (v)bende

cushion
(n) pillow, sitpillow, nielpillow (v) pillowe

custard
egcriem

custodian
kieper, upkieper, kerrtaeker

custody
kerr, waach, kieping, hoeld

custom
bewoent, duewway, sid

customary
bewoenlig, setwaylig

customer
cunder, shaaper

customs
toel, soeder

cut
(n) cut, snit (v) cutte, snyde

cuticle
outerskin

cutlet
cutling

cutter
cutter, snyder

cyanide
syanied

cycle
(n) crysloep, sykel (v) sykele

cyclone
wurlstorm, sycloen

cylinder
sylinder

cylindrical
sylindrish

cymbal
becken

cynic
syniker cynicalsynikish

cypress
sypres

cyst
sist

czar
kyser

Czech
Check

Czech Republic
Check Repueblic

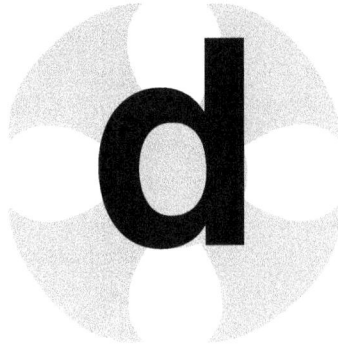

d

dad
daad, paap, paaw, daadie

daddy-long-legs
haarvestman, craenfly

daft
daft

daffodil
yelloew narsissus, daffodil

dagger
dagger, doelk

daily
daylig

dairy
milkwinkel, **dairy farm**- milkfaarm, derrie, milk-, derrie-

daisy
daysyger, yger av die day

dam
(n) dam, dyk (v) damme, damme off

damage
(n) shaad (v) beshaadige

damaging
beshaadig

dame
frouw, oeld frouw

damn
(n) fluck (v) dueme, ferdueme

damnable
duemlig, ferduemlig

damnation
duemness, ferduemness

damnatory
ferduemend

damp
damp

dampen
dampene, ferdampe

dance
(n) danz, (folk dance)-frick (v) danze, fricke

dancer
danzer

dandelion
lieowtand

Dane
Daan

danger
gefaar, freckness, haarmsway, plyt **danger zone**- gefaarzoen, haarmsway

dangerous
gefaarlig, frienig, frecken, plytlig

Danish
Daanish

dank
dank

dare
(n) derr, durf, getryst (v) derre, durve, waye

daring
(adj) derrend, durft (n) derring, tryst

dark
(adj) daark, murkig, donker (n) daark, murk, donker

darken
(vt)
daarkene, maeke daark, (vi) becueme(gette) daark

darkness
daarkness, murkigness, tiesterness, genip

darkroom
daarkruem

darling
(adj) lief, belueved, beluevd (n) daarling

darn
mende

dart
(n) daart, spierling (v) daarte

dash
(n) dash (v) dashe

data
(pl)daaten, gegivvens

date
(n) (time) daatum, tydpunt (social) offspreck (fruit) daadel (v) daterre, goewe out mid

daughter
daater

daughter-in-law
daater-in-laaw, laawdaater, shiendaater

dawn
(n) daan, daybraek, beginning (v) daane, beginne

day
day, **the day after tomorrow**- oevermorgen **the day before yesterday**- foeryester (day)

daybook
daybuek

daycare center
daykerrsenter

daydream
(n) daydriem (v) daydrieme

daylight
daylyt **daylight-saving time**- daylytsaavend tyd

daytime
daytyd, foerdaark

daze
(n) daes (v) daese

dazzle
(n) dassel, ferblinding (v) dassele, ferblinde

dazzling
dasslend

deacon
underpriest

dead
ded

deaden
deddene

deadliness
dedligness

deaf
deff, dief

deafen
deffene, maeke deff

deafness
deffness

deal
(n) diel (vt) diele (vi) diele mid

dean
dien

deanery
dienship

dear
dier

dearly
dierlig

death
det, (fig.) hienansyt

debatable
debaterrbaar

debate
(n) debaat (v) debaterre

debilitate
wiekene, swacke

debility
wiekness, swackness

debit
(n) debit (v) debiterre

debris
rubbel, debrie

debt
shuld, **be in debt-** bie fershulded, **be out of debt-** bie shuldfrie- **run into debt-** runne intue shuld

debug
unbugge, taeke away defects, beforse defects

decade
tenyiertyd

decaffeinated
cafienfrie

decapitate
behedde

decay
(n) ferfall, raating (v) ferfalle, raate

deceased
ded

decedent
dedling

deceit
bedraag, ieswyking, beswyking, foeken, swindel

deceitful
inwit,swindlig, beswyk, bedraagig

deceive
bedraage, misliede, swindele

December
Desember

decency
uprytness

deception
bedraagness. swindling

decide
beslisse, besluete, **decide that-** befinde dat

decimal
(adj) tendielig (n) tenbraek **decimal system-** tendielig setup, tendielig gestalt

decimate
slaatere, dessimerre, fernitte

decimation
slaater, dessimaassen, fernitting

decipher
unraadsele, unraavele

decision
beslissing, besluet

decisive
beslissend

deck
(n) deck (v) decke, naake doun

deck chair
foeldstuel, deckstuel

declaration
fercliering

declare
fercliere

declension
ferbouwing

decline
(n) (falling-off) ferfall (v) (fall off) ferfalle (gram) ferbouwe **decline with thanks-** betanke self

decode
= **decipher**

decompose
unbinde, raatte

decomposed
unbund, raated

decomposition
unbinding, raatting

decorate
smicke

decoration
smicking

decorator
smicker

decorous
smickig

decrease
(n) lessning, fermindring (v) lessene, fermindere, taeke away (av)

decree
(n) ferorder, decrie (v) ferordere, decrie

dedication
tuewyding

dedicate
tuewyde

deduct
taeke av, givve yn rebaat, (reasoning) besluete

deduction
(com) rebaat, prysdraap, taekoff (reasoning) besluet

deem
dieme

deep
diep

deepen
diepene

deepness
deepness, dept

deer
herrt

deface
maare

defacement
maaring

defamation
illspeech

defame
speeke ill av

defeat
(n) nedderlay (v) winne oever(or agenst), nedderlaye, ferslaye, oevercueme

defect
(n) shortcueming, mangel, falt, flaaw, defect (v) cueme short, lacke, falle away, ferlette, deserterre

defection
wayfall

defective
mangelful, lackend

defectiveness
mangelfulness, unfullcuemingness

defend
ferdeddige, widstande, fiete back, stande taegen

defendant
beshuldigd

defender
ferdeddiger

defense
ferdeddiging, wid- taegenstand

defensible
ferdeddigbaar

defensive
ferdeddiglig, (psych.) defensiv

defer 1
putte off, hoelde back

defer 2
yelde (tue)

deference
acting, oerbieding

deferment
putoff, hoeldback

defiance
outdaying, boeldness

defiant
outdayend, boeld, braesen

deficiency
lack, shortcueming, shortfall

deficit
geldshortfall

defile
beflecke, bewemme, besmutte, befoule

defilement
beflecking, bewemming, besmutting, befouling

define
defineere, fercleere

definite
foerset, cleer, secker, bestemmed,(gram.) begrensend

deflate
lette dee luft out, flattene

deflation
(econ) deflaassen

deform
misforme, misshaepe

deformed
misformed, misshaepen

deformity
misshaepenness

defraud
bedrigge, swindele, besteele, tricke

defray
becoste

defrost
unfroste

deft
deft

degradation
stepferloewring, degraading

degrade
stepferloewere, degraade

degrading
stepferloewrend, degraadend

degree
(measurement)-graad, step (educ) degree (social) rung **degrees (small amt)**- bits, steplings

deification
fergodding

deify
fergodde

deity
godness, god, goddess

dejected
bedruckt

dejection
bedrucktness

delay
(n) putoff, hoeldback, bedraaging (v) putte off, hoelde back, bedraage, draage oens feet

delegate
(n) forstander, forspeeker (v) benaeme

delegation
forstanderhud, dellegaassen

delete
strieke out, rubbe out, taeke(nieme) out

deletion
striekout, rubout, taekout, niemout

deliberate
(adj) sloew, langsum, by steps, foertot, foerplanned (vi) fertinke (vt) tinke oever, waye oever

deliberation
fertinking

delicate
sliet, braekbaar, fien, week, brittel

delicious
lecker. gudsmacklig

delight
(n) behaag (v) taeke(nieme) behaag in

delightful
behaaglig

delinquency
oevertiedshuld, unfullfill- ing, falt, misdeed

delinquent
(adj) oevertiedig, deedfaelig (n) wrangduewer, **juvenile deliquent**- teeenwrangduewer

delirious
mad, craesee, madsensig, mindtrillend

delirium
madness, craeseeness, madsensigness, mind-trillendness

deliver
(release)befree, sette free, gefrelse ferluese, (a speech)- uttere, (mail) berre, bringe, (transfer)-hande oever

deliverance
befreeing, ferluesing

delivery
berring

dell
dell

delude
misleede, tricke, ferblende

deluge
graet flued, hevvig raen, aan oeverwelming, graet number, oeverfloewing

delusion
ferblending, trick, (psych.) deluesen

delve
delve

demagog
demmagoeg

demagogic
demmagoegish

demand
(n) ferlangen, fordring (v) ferlange, fordere

demanding
fordrend

demean
fermeene, ferloewere, (behavior)- benieme self, hoelde self

demeaning
fermeenend, ferloewrend

demeanor
selfhoelding, selfbenieming

dementia
loss av goestig miet, goestig mietloss

demerit
falt, shortcueming, widmaark, taegenmaark

demobilize
demoebiliseere, unbeweppene

demobilization
demoebiliseering, unbeweppning

democracy
demmocratee

democrat
demmocrat

demonstrable
bewiesbaar, shoewbaar

demonstrate
bewiese, shoewe, beswuetele

demonstration
bewiesing, shoewing, beswuetling

demonstrative
bewieslig, outshoewend, beswuetlig, (gram.)- onwiesend, betoeknend

demonstrator
shoewer, maarcher

denial
fernoewing, bestriet, wid-, taegensaying, unoewing

denizen
bewoener

denominate
benaeme, calle

denomination
benaeming, (rel.)-sect, confessionell, (fin.)- naemweurt

denominator
naemer

denounce
brande, foerdueme

dense
tick

denseness
tickness

dent
dent

dental
tand-, tandish

dentist
tandloeker

denude
maeke berr, laye berr, strippe

denunciation
branding, foerdueming

denial
unkenning, ferloekning

deny
unsaye, loekene, benecke, unkenne, widsacke, sacke taegen, bestriete, gaensaye

deodorant
smellmiddel, gudbesmelling, smellbeniemer

deodorize
smellbenieme

depart
goewe away, leeve, sette out(av), resse av, ferferre, (fig)dye

department
offdeeling, depaartment

departure
leeving, waygang, offress

depend
hange on , leene on, (trust)- truste, fertrouwe

dependable
fertrouwbaar, trouwful, trouwweurdig

dependability
trouwfulness, fertrouwbaarness,
trouwweurdigness

dependant
= **dependent**

dependent
(n) onleener, kinhanger (adj) onleenend,
onhangend

depict
bewriete

depilatory
unherringsmiddel

deplete
feremptige, ferbrueke

depopulate
unfoelke

deport
sende away (off), deporteere

deposit
deponeere

depot
werrhous, traenstaassen, busstaassen

depreciate
luese weurt, weurtlessene, weurtfermindere

depreciation
weurtloss, weurtlessning, weurtfermindring

depress
drucke nedder, bedrucke, (med.) depresseere

depressed
(med.) depresseered

depression
bedruckedness, (med.) depressen

deprivation
bedelling, benieming,

beroeving

deprive
bedelle, benieme, beroeve, beneete,
taeke(nieme) frum

depth
dept, deepness

deride
laffe at, maeke fun av, ferlaffe, bespotte

derision
bespotting, hoen, ferlaffing

derisive
spottend, hoenend,
ferlaffig

derivation
offleeding, ordfrummer

derivative
(adj) offled (n) offleed

derive
leede off(frum), cueme frum

descend
cueme doun, goewe doun, stiege off,
clieme doun, cueme after, folge, folloewe

descendant
= **descendent**

descendent
(adj) folgend (n) aftercuemer, folger

describe
bewriete

description
bewrieting

descriptive
bewrietend

desecrate
unhoelige, unwiede

desecration
unhoeliging. unwieding

desert 1
fersaeke, ferlette, flee

desert 2
waestland, wilderness, dryland

deserter
deseurter, fleeyer

desertion
ferletness, fliet

deserve
ferdeene

deserving
weurdig, ferdeenend

design

(n) plan, setup, layout, drauwup, unwerrp
(v) planne, sette up, laye out, drauwe up,
unwerrpe

designate
benaeme. betoekene

designation
benaeming, betoekning

designer
sketcher

desirable
wenslig

desire
(n) willning, wens, wish, yerrning, craeving (v)
willene, wense, wishe, ferlange, yerrne wille
tue, craeve

desirous of
ferlangend tue

desk
wriettish, weurktish, weurkseet

desolate
(n) loenlig, unfoelked, unhappig, ferduen (v)
laye waest, fersaeke, maeke unhappig

despair
(n) unhoep, hoeploss, hoeplessness (v)
unhoepe, luese hoep

despairing
hoepless, unhoepig

despise
feracte, oeverhoege, haete, loede

despite
nitwidstandend, trots

dessert
aftermeel(sweets)

destination
bestemming

destine
bestemme

destined
bestemmed

destiny
bestemming

destitute
oeveraarm, fersaeken

destroy
ferduewe, terrfalle, tuewerrpe, ferspille,
bemyere, unduewe, fernitte, tueslaye

destruction
ferdeed, tieberness, fernitting, ferspilling,
terrfall, tuewerrping

detail
(n) (no pl.) ondelness, detell (v) givve
ondelness (detells)

detain
hoelde up(back), bestoppe, behalte, hoelde,
ferbiede

detect
undecke, finde out, unhiede

detection
undecking, unhieding

detective
unberiddler, detectiv detective story-
criminallromaan

detector
undecker, unhieder

detention
hoeldup, hoeldback, ferbieding

deter
shricke av ,
skerre av

detergent
clensingmiddel, waashmiddel

deteriorate
ferweurse, weursene

deterioration
ferweursing, weursning

determination
besliet

determine
besliete

detest
haete, loede

dethrone
untroene

detonate
fertundere, exploderre, sette off

detonation
fertundring, settoff

detour
imway

detract
taeke (nieme) back, lessene, clienere

detriment
shaad, haarm

detrimental
shaadish, haarmful

devalue
lessene dee weurt av, weurtlessene

devaluation
weurtlessning

devastate
ferwilde, laye wild, ferduewe, maeke helpless, oeverwelme

devastating
haartbraekend, oeverwelmend

devastation
ferwilding

develop
unfolde, unwickele, unwrappe

developer
unfoelder, unwickler

developing
unfoeldend, unwicklend

development
unfoelding, unwickling

deviant
offwiekend

deviate
(n) offwieker (v) offwieke, turne asied

deviation
offwieking

device
tuel, plan

devil
devvil, Saatan

devilish
devvilish

devious
offwayig, misleedend

devise
tinke up (out), planne, becrafte

devoid of
emptig av

devote
sette asied, givve self tue, tuewiede self on

devoted
luevend, trouwfast, trouwful

devotion
tuewieding, devotions- gebeds

devour
freete

devout
godluevend, eurnest, haartfelt

dew
duew

dexterous
behandig, tweehandskilled

dexterity
behandigness, tweehandskill

diabetes
suegersickness, hybluedsueger

diabetic
(adj) suegersick (n) suegersickling

diabolic(al)
devvilig, Saatanig

diagnose
untangele, unravvele, besundere

diagnosis
untangling, unravvling, besundring

diagonal
(adj, n)
diagonall

diagram
diagraam, skeem

dial
(n) disk, shoewplaat (v) befingere

dialect
undertall, underspeech, dialect

dialectal
undertallig, dialectish

dialog(ue)
tweespeech, dialoeg

diameter
middellien

diamond
diamaant

diaper
litlingwrap

diaphragm
midriff

diarrhea
falldrue, luesstuel

diary
daybuek

dice
gambelstoen

dictate
(n) behest (v) beherre, dicterre

dictation
dicterring

dictator
dictaater

dictatorial
dictaatrish

dictatorship
dictaatership, dictaatur

diction
weurdbruek

dictionary
weurdbuek

die 1
dye

die 2
gambelstoens

diet
(n) dyet (v) dyete, folge(folloewe) aan dyet

differ
fershille, be unliek

difference
fershill, unliekness,
undersheed

different
fershillend, un(a)liek, undersheedend

differentiate
undersheede

difficult
haard, sweerig, aarfed, lastig, ferswerrlig

difficulty
haardship, aarfedness, sweerigness,
ferswerrligness

diffuse
spredde out, ferspredde

diffusion
ferspredding

dig
(n) dig (v) digge, (fig) delve

digging
digging

digest
(n) fersaamling, fergaddring (v) fersaamele,
fergaddere, swaaloewe, swelge

digestible
swaaloewbaar, swelgenbaar

digestion
swaaloewing, swelging

digit
finger, siefer

digital
fingrig, siefrig

dignified
weurdig

dignify
ferweurdige

dignitary
hyfoelk

dignity
weurdigness, oer

dike
diek

dilapidated
ferfallen

dilapidation
ferfall

dilate
ferwiedere, beswelle

dilation
ferwiedring, beswelling

dilemma
dilemma

diligence
giemen, iever

diligent
flietig, emsig

diligently
flietig, emsig, mid giemen

dill
dill

dilute
fertinne, weekene

dim
dim

dime
teenter, teenthundred

dimension
offmeet, imfang

diminish
lessene, fermindere, fersmallere, ferclienere

diminutive
ferclienerweurd

dimple
dimpel

din
(n) din (v) dinne

dine
eete

diner
eeter, eethous

dining room
eetruem, eetsall

dinner
eevningmeel, (main meal) swaesen

dint
dint

dip
(n) dip (v) dippe

diphtheria
difteeria

diphthong
tweeclink

diploma
diploem

diplomacy
diplomaatee

diplomat
diplomaat

diplomatic
diplomaatish

diplomatically
diplomaatish

dipper
dipper

dipstick
dipstick

dire
dredful, feer- arousend, shricklig, dringend

direct
(adj) straet, direct (v) leede, wisse, besteere

directly
straet(a)way

direction
way, _s rietings

directive
besteering, directiv

director
leeder, directer

dirt
deurt

dirtiness
deurtigness

dirty
deurtig, befouled, smutttig

disability
unfermayen, unbecwaamness

disable
crippele, maeke unweurkbaar

disabled
crippeled, unbewaybaar **the disabled**- dee behindered

disadvantage
afterdeel, draawback, haarm, hindring, handicap

disadvantageous
afterdeelig, haarmful, hindrish

disagree
nit stemme oeveroen, nit be av oen mind, (food) sickene

disagreeable
(weather) unangenaem (people) unbehaaglig

disagreement
unoenigness, be unoenig

disallow
unlette, unferleeve

disappear
ferswinde, beferre

disappearance
ferswind, beferring

disappoint
unferblisse, unbedraage, untoushe

disappointing
unferblissend, unbedraagig

disappointment
unferbliss, unbedraaging, un- toushing, widfall

disapproval
untaeving, unbilliging

disapprove
untaeve, unbillige

disarm
unweppene

disarmament
unweppning

disassemble
taeke(nieme) asunder

disaster
catastroef, ramp

disavow
nit bekenne,
nit andette, loekene

disband
unbinde

disbelief
unbeleef

disburse
givve out

disbursement
outgivving

disc
(anat) shief (sport) discus (music) disk

discard
ferwerrpe, troewe away, gette rid av, ferridde

discharge
(n) fyring, unhyring, unletting, (med.) outdrift, outfloew (v) (dismiss) fyere, unhyere unloede. befree, luesene

disciple
Cristfolger, Cristfollower, Cristfrend, apostel

disciplinarian
orderkeeper

disciplinary
bestraffig, tintrig

discipline
orderkeeping, teedship

disclose
unwrappe, unhiede, undecke, maeke bekent

disclosure
unwrapping, unhieding

discolor
ferfaarbe

discoloration
ferfaarbing

disconnect
unplugge, unferbinde

discontent
ungesaelig, un- lucklig, unhappig

discontinuance
stopping, givvingup

discontinuation
= **discontuance**

discontinue
stoppe, givve up, braeke up, stoppe + -en inf
(e.g. He did stoppe weurken derr.)

discord
unoenigness, lack av oenmindness,
unoeveroenstemming, (mus.) haarmoneelack,
unhaarmonee, misclink

discotheque
discotec

discount
(n) loewring, priesloewring (v) loewere dee
pries, selle for less, nit beleeve

discourage
unmuedige, unhaartene

discouragement
unmuedigness

discover
undecke, finde out, feurstfinde

discoverer
undecker, feurstfinder

discovery
undecking, feurstfind

discredit
(n) twievel, miscreddit, trustloss (v) bringe
twievel (miscreddit, trustloss) on

discreet
ferseckrig, kerrful, discreet

discrepancy
fershill, unstemmigness

discretion
kerr, discreeten, tact, beslissingcraft

discretionary
beslissingcraftig,
discreetnish

discriminate
undersheede,
shoewe foerdeeming

discrimination
undersheed, foerdeeming

discriminatory
undersheedend, foerdeemingful

discuss
bespeeke, talke oever(about), behandele

discussion
bespeeking , talk

disease
sickness, illness, oedel

diseased
sick

disembowel
taeke (cutte) out dee innerdeels

disenchant
sette free av mistaeken (fals) beleef (illuesen)

(be) disenchanted with
haarbere (hoelde) noew illuesens oever

disengage
(vt) luesene (vi) luesene self

disfavor
ungenaad

disfiguration
= **disfigurement**

disfigure
shende, unstelle

disfigurement
shending, unstelling

disgrace
(n) shaem, ungenaad (v) beshaeme, bringe in
ungenaad , bringe shaem on

disgraceful
shaemful

disguise
(n) ferbluem. fermomming, ferstelling,
fercladding (v) ferblueme, fermomme,
ferstelle, fercladde

disgust
(n) loeding, aekel, walging (v) sickene, aekele-
be disgusted with(at)- be sickened (aekeled)
by, walgene av

dish
shoetel, plaet

dishearten
unmuedige, unhaartene

dishonest
unoerlig , unredlig

dishonesty
unoerligness, unredligness

dishonor
(n) shaem, unoer, oerlessness, oerlack (v)
bringe shaem(unoer) on, beshaeme

dishonored
unbeoered, oerbeniemed

dishcloth
shoetelcloet, shoetelrag

dish towel
shoeteltouwel

dishwasher
shoetelwaasher

dishwater
shoetelwaater

disillusion
unsoeber, unnuctere **be disillisioned with**-
be unsoebered (unnuctered) mid, haarbere
(hoelde) noew illuesens oever

disinclination
ungeniegedness

disinclined
ungenieged, unwillend

disinfect
unbekieme, disinfecterre

disinfectant
unbekiemer, unbekiemmiddel,
disinfecteermiddel

disinherit
unerrve

disintegrate
terrfalle, braeke up, falle asunder, unbinde

disintegration
terrfall, asunderfall, braekup, unbinding

disinter
digge up

disinterest
unbelang, belanglessness

disinterested
belangless

disk See
disc.

dislike
(n) unlieking (v) nit lieke

dislocate
unwricte, pulle out, wrenche

dislocation
unwricting, wrenching

disloyal
untrouwful, untrouwfast

disloyalty
untrouwfulness, untrouwfastness

dismal
daark, gluemig, dull

dismantle
taeke(nieme) asunder, terre doun

dismay
(n) muedloss, muedlessness, hoeploss,
hoeplessness

dismember
cutte av lims, benieme oen av membership,
unlimmme

dismiss
lette leeve, sende away, fyere, unhyere, nit
heede

dismissal
leeving, fyring, unhyring

disobedience
ungehyersumness, unheersumness

disobedient
ungehyersum, unheersum

disobey
ungehyersumme, unheersumme, unbehorke

disorder
unorder

disorderly
unorderlig

disorganization
disorganisaassen

disorganize
disorganiserre

disorganized
disorganiserred

disown
unoewne

disparity
uneevenness

dispassionate
calm, feelingless, unfeelend, unpaarteeish

dispel
drieve away (av)

dispensary
apoteek

dispensation
befreeing,
ferdeeling

dispense
givve out, deele out, free av, **dispense with**-
gette rid av, duewe away mid

dispersal
ferspredding, scattring

disperse
spredde out, ferspredde, scattere

displace
upruete, ferdringe, (replace)- ferfange

displaced
uprueted, ferdringed

displacement
uprueting, ferdringing, (replacement)-
ferfanging

display
(n) showeing, fertoening, shoewingoff (v)
shoewe, fertoene, shoewe av

displease
mishaage, ungecweeme, ungelicke

displeasure
mishaag

disposable
(adj) waytroewbaar, ferridbaar (n) troewaway

disposal
beshicking

dispose
beshicke, **dispose of**- troewe away, gette rid av,
ferridde

disposition
mindset, mued, ferridding

disproportion
uneevenness

disproportionate
uneevenlig -ly -uneevenlig

disprove
nuewlaye, shoewe tue be wrang

disputable
beflitbaar, betwistbaar disputant beflitter

dispute
(n) beflit, dispuet, striet (v) beflitte, betwiste.
disputerre

disqualification
geckel, discwalificaassen

disqualify
geckele, discwalifikerre

disregard
(n) unheed (v) nit givve heed tue, givve noew
heed tue

disrepair
ferfall

disreputable
ferruefen

disrepute
ill ruef, ill naem

disrespect
unoerbiedigness, unacting, unhoffligness

disrespectful
unoerbiedig, unactingful, unhofflig

disrobe
uncladde self, taeke off claddings, benieme
claddings

disrupt
braeke up, braeke in on, ferbraeke

disruption
ferbraeking

disruptive
ferbraekish

dissatisfaction
untuefridness

dissatisfy
nit befriddige

dissatisfying
unbefriddigend

dissect
taeke(cutte) asunder,
unlimme

dissection
unlimming

disseminate
scattere, spredde, soewe

dissemination
scattring, spredding, soewing

dissension
unoenigness, ferdeelness, wrangling

dissent
wrangele, be av ander mind, fershille, tinke
fershillend

dissenter
andertinker

dissertation
dissertaassen

disservice
undeenst

dissever
cutte (sniede) av

dissident
andertinkender

dissimilar
unliek, unaliek, fershillend

dissimilarity
unliekness, fershill

dissipate
drieve away, ferdrieve, scatter, scwaandere

dissolubility
luesenbaarness, braekupness, melting

dissoluble
luesenbaar, meltbaar, unbindbaar

dissolvable
=**dissoluble**

dissolve
luesene, braeke up, melt, unbinde

dissyllabic
tweesilbenlig

distance
(n) faarness, faaroffness, offstand (v) stande
aluef frum, stande self away av

distant
faar, faaroff

distasteful
unsmacklig

distemper
illness, sickness, hundsickness

distinct
feshillend, fersheedend

distinction
undersheed, asunder- setting,bekentness

distinctive
maarkbaar

distinctiveness
maarkbaarness

distinguish
telle fershill between, undersheede, maeke self
maarkbaar

distinguished
well noewn, beruemt, bekent, getungen

distinguishable
undersheedbaar

distort
twiste, wriggele, ferwringe

distortion
twisting, ferwrungnness

distract
draawe away, mindwaandere

distraction
ferdraawing, mindwaandring

distribute
ferdeele, hande out, sende out, givve out

distribution
ferdeeling

distributor
ferdeeler

district
shyer

distrust
(n) untrouw, mistrouw (v) untrouwe,
mistrouwe

distrustful
untrouwish, mistrouwish

disturb
stoere, ferunruewige, braeke dee ruew (frid)

disturbance
stoering, unruew, unfrid

disturbing
ferstoerend

disunion
unoenigness

disunite
becueme unoenig

disunited
unferoeniged

disuse
(n) unbruek **fall into disuse**- falle intue
unbruek

ditch
ditch

ditto
(n) dee saem, copee (v) copeere, maeke copees
av (adv) liekwies

diuretic
(n) waaterpill, urinerrmiddel (adj) befloewend,
urinbefloewend

dive
(n) diev, ferdoun (v) dieve, ferdoune

diver
diever, ferdouner

diverge
turne off (away), belimme

divergence
belimming, wayturning

diverse
missenlitch, fersheeden, fershillend

diversification
ferandring, fersheeding

diversify
fersheede, belimme

diversion
(amusement) fermaek, tiedpasser, ferandring

diversity
fersheedenness

divert
turne asied, offwende

divide
ferdeele, divideere, splitte,**divide up**- splitte
up, sherre

dividend
sherrbetalling, (math) deelnumber, dividend

divider
deeler,sunderer

divine
(adj) godtrouwfast, godliek (n) goestliger,
godtaen (v) truetfinde, foertelle

divinity
godtrouwfastness, godliekness, godcraft,
godkennis

divisibility
deelbaarness

divisible
deelbaar

division
ferdeeling, ferdeelness

divisor
deeler

divorce
(n) unwedlock, wedsundring, yiftsundring

divulge
unhiede, maeke noewn

do
duewe

docile
gewillig, folgensum, leedsum

dock 1
(n) (wharf) dock (v) docke

dock 2
(court) dock

dock 3
(weed) dock

dock 4
(animal tail) dock

doctor
loeker, doctor, heeler

doctorate
doctoraat

doctrine
teeching, hoeldings

document
(n) pruefwrit (v) prueve, befande, bewiese

documentary
(adj) documentrig (e,g, documentrig bewiesing) (n) documentaar

dodge
(n) dodg, dodging (v) dodge

doe
doew

doer
duewer

dog
hund

dogma
dogma, beleefs

domestic
(adj) inlandish, inland..., houshoeldish, houshoeld..., houslig (n) houskeeper, maed

dominance
oeverherrsing, beherrsing

dominant
(adj) oeverherrsend (n) (genetics, music)- dominant

dominate
(vt) beherrse, touwere oever (vi) herrse, hoelde sway

domination
herrship

domineer
oeverherrse, brouwbeete, bullee

domineering
oeverberrend, oeverherrsend

Dominican
Dominniker

dominion
herrship, sway

domino
doeminoew

donate
shenke, givve

donation
shenking, gift

donkey
donkee, aesel

donor
shenker,givver **blood donor**- bluedshenker

doom
(n) duem (v) dueme

doomsday
duemsday

door
doer

doorway
doerway, ingang, inway

dormant
sleepend, ruewend

dormitory
stuedenthall, lerrnerhall, sleephall dot dot

double
(n) tweefoeld, twin, dubbel (baseball)- tweebaager, **double standard**- tweekindmaat, (v) betwinne, ferdubbele

doubt
(n) tween, twievel (v) tweene, betwievele

doubtful
tweenful, twievlish

dough
doew

doughty
doutig

dove
duev

down 1
(adv) doun, dounway

down 2
(n) (feathers, fine hair)- doun

down 3
(n) (open, grassy land)- doun

downfall
dounfall

dowry
widdoewgift

dowse 1
(naut) douse

dowse 2
douse

dowser
douser

dowsing
dousing

doze
doese

dozen
twelvsum, twelvset, duesen

drab
yelloewbroun, dull, oentoenig
draft (n) draft (v) drafte

drag
(n) draag (v) draage

drain
(n) draen (v) draene

drainage
(process) draening (system) draenpieps (waste) draenings

drake
draek

drama
draama

dramatic
dramaatish

dramatist
dramaatiker

dramatize
dramaatiserre

drape
(n) foerhang, luesfoelds (v) becladde, hange, foeldhange

draper
dryguedshandler, dryguedsdeeler

drastic
haarsh

draw
(n) draaw (v) draawe

drawer
droer

drawing
draawing

drawl
drall, sloew speechway

dray
(n) dray (v) draye

dread
(adj) dred, aawsum (n) dred (v) dredde
dream (n) dreem (v) dreeme

drear
(poet) dreer

dreary
dreerig

dreariness
dreerigness

dredge 1
(n) dredg (v) dredge

dredge 2
(cuisine) dredge

dregs
dregs

drench
drenche

dress
(adj) dress (n) dress, claddings (v) dresse, cladde self dribble (n) dribbel (v) dribbele

drift
(n) drift (v) drifte

drifter
drifter

drift-ice
drifties

driftwood
driftwud

drill 1
(n) (tool) drill (v) drille

drille 2
(n) (furrow, machine making furrows)- drill
(v) (plant) drille

drille 3
(linen, cotton twill)- drill

drille 4
(monkey) - drill

drink
(n) drink (v) drinke drip (n) drip (v) drippe
drippings drippings drippy drippig drive (n)
driev (v) drieve

drive-in
drievin drivel (n) drivvel (v) drivvele driven
(adj) drivven, - drivven

driver
driever

drive shaft
drievshaft

drive-up
drievup

drive-through
drievtrue

driveway
drievway

drizzle
(n) drissel (v) drissele

dromedary
oenhumpcamell

drone 1
(n) (non-worker) droen (v) (not work) droene

drone 2
(n) (sound) droen (v) (sound) droene

drool
(n) druel (v) druele

droop
(n) druep (v) druepe

droopy
druepig

drop
(n) drop, dropoff (v) droppe (av)

droppings
droppings

droplet
dropling

dropsy
waaterswelling

dross
dross

drought
drout, drytied, waaterlack, lack

drove
droev

drover
droever

drown
droune, (fig.) ferdrinke

drowning
drouning

drowse
(n) drous (v) drouse

drowsy
drousig

drowsiness
drousigness

drudge
(n) drudg (v) drudge

drudgery
drudgness

drug
(n) droeg, naarcoetic (v) droege

drug addict
droegclinger droegbrueker

druggist
apoteeker, droegist

drug store
apoteek, droegwinkel

drum
drum

drunk
(adj) drunk (n) drunk

drunkard
drunker

drunken
drunken

dry
(adj) dry (v) drye

dry cell
drysell

dry-clean
drycleene

dry dock
(n) drydock (v) drydocke

dryer
dryer

dry goods
drygueds

dryness
dryness

dry wall
drywall

dual
(adj) tweefoeld

dualism
tweefoeldness

duality
= dualism

dub
dubbe

dubious
tweenful, twievlish

duck 1
(fowl) duck, (masc) draek

duck 2
ducke

duck 3
(cloth) duck duct piep, piepweurk

ductile
stretchbaar, bendbaar, shaepbaar, formbaar

dud
dud

due
oewed, fallig, betallbaar

duet
duwet, tweesumsang, tweesumsingers

dull
dull

dumb
dum

dummy
dummee

dump
(n) dump (v) dumpe

dumpling
dumpling

dun 1
(adj) dun, graybroun (n) dun, graybroun,
(horse) dun

dun 2
dunne

dung
(n) dung, shaarn (v) dunge

dungeon
undergrundhefthoeld, undergrundfengness

duo
tweesum

dupe
misleede

duplicate
(n) twin, dubbel (v) betwinne, ferdubbele

duplicity
twindeeling

durability
lastbarness

durable
lastbaar

duration
lastness

duress
dwang

during
wielen

dusk
dusk, nietfall, feurstdaark

dust
dust

dusty
dustig

Dutch
(adj) Hollandish, Nedderlandish (n)
(language) Hollandish, (person) Hollander,
Nedderlander

dutiful
oerbiedig, plicttrouwful

duty
plict

dwarf
dwaarf, dworf

dwell
dwelle

dwelling
dwelling

dwindle
dwindele

dye
(n) dy, faarben (v) dye, faarbene

dynamic
dinaamish, mietlaeden

dynamics
dinaamics

dynamite
(n) dinamiet (v) dinamiete, bloewe up

dynasty
dinastee

dysentery
ruer

dystrophy
ferdwindling

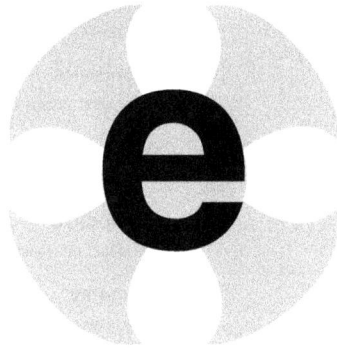

e

each
eech

each other
eechander

eager
fierig, iefrig, yerrnful, ferlangen

eagerness
iever, ferlangen, yerrnfulness

eagle
errn

eagelet
errnling

ear
eer

eardrum
eerdrum

earl
errl

earliness
errligness, tiedligness

early
errlig, tiedlig, frueg

earn
errne, ferdeene

earnest
errnest

earnestly
errnestlig

earnestness
errnst

earnings
errnings, ferdeenings

earring
eerring

earth
errt

earthen
errten

earthenware
errtenwerr

earthquake
errtcwaek

ease
(n)(comfort)- behaag, gemaak, (without difficulty)- unaarfedness (v) lietene (up), **ease off**- lette up

easel
eesel

easiness
unaarfedness

east
eest

Easter
Eester

eastern
eestern

eastward
eestway

easy
liet, unaarfed, nit haard

eat
eete, **eat up**- eete up

eatable
eetbaar

eatables
eetwerrs

eaves
eevs

eavesdrop
eevesdroppe, lissene in on

ebb
(n) eb (v) ebbe

ebbtide
ebtied

ebonite
eebeniet

ebony
eebenholt

eccentric
(adj) ecsentrish (n) ecsentriker

eccentricity
ecsentrishness

ecclesiastic
goestlig, keurklig

echo
(n) backsteeven, eccoew, afterclink (v) eckoewe, back- steevene

echoic
eckoewish, backsteevnish

eclipse
(n) eclips, sunhieding, muenhieding (v) dimme, darkene

ecological
ecoloegish

ecologist
ecoloeg

ecology
ecoloegee

economical
= **economic**

economic
triftig, econoemish, sperrsum

economics
triftcraft, econoemics

economist
triftcrafter, econoemiker

economize
betrifte, economerre

economy
trift, econoemee

ecstasy
oeverbliss, ecstaasee

ecstatic
oeverblissig, ecstaatig

ecumenical
ecumennish

ecumenism
ecumenness

eddy
eddig, weurl

edge
(n) edg, rand (v) edge

edgeways
edgways

edgewise
var. of **edgways**

edging
edging

edgy
edgig

edible
eetbaar

edict
ferorder, decree, behest

edifice
gebouw

edification
inlietning, upbouwing

edify
inlietene, bouwe up

edit
editte, redigerre, foerchecke, besorgene

edition
edissen, outgav

editor
editter, besorger

editorial
leedaartikel, hedaartikel, edittertaat(s)

editorship
edittership

educate
bewitte, fostere, getee

education
bewitting, fostring

educational
bewittig, fostrig

educator
bewitter, teecher, belerrner, geteer

eel
eel

efface
wiepe out

effect
(n)outcuem, outweurk, ferfolging, outgroet (v) bringe about, beweurke

effective
weurksum

effeminate
wievish, ferwieft, frouwish

effervesce
bubbele (up), fisse, foeme

effervescent
bubblend, fissend

effervescence
bubbels, foem

efficiency
weurking, output, forttoegishsness, fortbring, akennishness

efficient
weurksum,forttoegish, fortbrigend, akennish

effigy
lieknessling, liekling, underliekness

effort
inspanning

effortless
sonder inspanning, inspanningless

effrontery
illboeldness, unshaem

effuse
spredde (sende) out, spredde (sende) fort

effusion
outspredding(-sending), (fortspredding (-sending)

effusive
outsendlig, fortsendlig

eft
eft

e.g.
b.s. (byspell), f.b. (foerbild)

egg
eg

egg-nog
egnog

eggshell
egshell

ego
dee self, eegoew, selfloff

egocentric
selfmiddeled, eegoewsentrish

egoism
ickness, selfloff, eegoewsenteredness, selfmiddeledness, selfcraeving

egoist
= egotist

egoistic
= egotistic

egomania
eegoewsickness

egomaniac
eegoewsickling

egotism
= egoism

egotist
selfloffer, selfcraever eegoewtist

egotistic
selfloffend, selfcraevend, eegoewtistish

ego trip
eegoewtrip

Egypt
Eegipt

Egyptian
1. (person) Eegipter (adj)Eegiptish 2.(language of ancient Egyptians) -Eegiptish

eiderdown
iederdoun

eight
ect

eighteen
ectteen

eighteenth
ectteent

eighth
ectter

eighty
ecttig

either
eeder (oen)

ejaculate
druste out, spille, eyaculerre

ejaculation
outdrust, spilling, eyaculaassen

eject
troewe out, ferdrieve

ejection
troewout, ferdrieving

elaborate
(adj)oeverlaeden, bedecked (v)weurke out, speeke fullig, speeke at lengt, unfoelde, unwrappe, givve ondelness (detells)

elaboration
unfoelding, unwrapping

eland
eeland

elapse
ferloepe, goewe by

elastic
elastish

elasticity
elastishness

elate
uplifte, lifte up

elation
upliftendness

elbow
(n)elboew (v) elboewe oens way

elbowroom
elboewruem

eld
eld

elder
(adj) elder (n)elder

elderly
elderlig, beyeered

eldest
eldest, moest elderlig

elect
(n) dee choesen (v) ferchuese

election
ferchuesing

elective
(n) chuesing (adj) choesen

elector
chueser

electoral
chueser-

elctoral college
chueserhud

electorate
chuesership

electric
electrish

electrical
= **electric**

electrician
electriker

electricity
electricness

electrification
electriserring

electrify
electriserre

electrocardiogram
electro- caardiogram

electrocardiograph
electro- caardiograaf

electrocute
electrokille

electrocution
electrokilling

electrode
electroed

electrolysis
electrolissis, electroluesning

electrolyze
electrolisse, electroluesene

electromagnet
electromagnet

electromagnetic
electromagnettish

electron
electroen

electronic
electroenish

elegance
befalligness, ellegans

elegant
befallig, ellegant, gesmackful

elegy
waelsang, moernsang, sorgensang

element
ellement, bestanddeel **elements (basic)**-
beginsels

elemental
ellementrish

elementary
ellementrish, **elementary school**- grundscuel,
loewscuel

elephant
ellefant

elephantine
ellefantish, oevergraet

elevate
lifte up, uplifte, raese, hietene

elevated
lifted up, raesed, uplifted, hy, hietened

elevation
loftiness, hiet, raesing

elevator
lift, lifter

eleven
elv

eleventh
elft

elf
elf

elfin
elfin

elicit
drauwe out, unlocke

elide
leeve out, slurre oever

eligibility
ferchuesbaarness

eligible
ferchuesbaar, berietig, (--bachelor) wedbaar,

eliminate
taeke out, nieme out, leeve out, gette rid av,
duewe away mid, ferridde

elimination
(niem-) taekout, leevout, ferridding,
ferwaying

elite
ferbest, eleet, hyfolk

elitism
ferbestness, eleetness

elk
elk, waapetee

ellipse
(geom) elips

ellipsis
elipsis

elliptical
eliptish

elm
elm

elocution
speekcraft, speechcraft

elongate
lengtene, ferlenge

elongation
lengtning, ferlenging

elope
eloepe

elopement
eloeping

eloquence
wellspeekendness

eloquent
wellspeekend

else
els

elsewhere
elswerr

elude
gette free, gette away, runne away, sneeke av
(away), steele away, shunne, flee

elusion
eluesen

elusive
haardfangbaar, haardgraspbaar

elusory
= **elusive**

emaciate
ferleene, fermeegere

emaciated
ferleened, fermeegered

emaciation
ferleening, fermeegring

emanate
streeme out, cueme av, cueme fort, floewe av

emanation
outstreeming, outfloewing, fortcueming

emancipate
free, befree, sette free, emanciperre

emancipation
freeing, emancipaassen

emasculate
unmanne

emasculation
unmanning

embalme
balseme

embalming
balseming

embank
bedieke

embankment
bedieking

embargo
(n) embaargoew, baaring (v) shutte av, baare,
embaargoewe

embark
putte abord, goewe abord, beginne, sette out
for, leeve for, borde

embarkation
onset, bording

embarrass
maeke ferlayen, fershye, beshaeme

embarrassed
beshaemed, ferlayen, fershied

embarrassment
ferlayenness, fershyness

embassy
boedberrderhous, errendberrderhous

embed
inbedde, inlaye

embellish
fersheene, bedecke

embellishment
fersheening, bedecking

ember
ember

embezzle
steele, understeele, underslaye

embezzlement
understeeling, underteft, underslaying

embezzler
understeeler, underteef, underslayer

embitter
ferbittere

embitterment
ferbittring

emblem
toekenbild

embody
beliecaame

embodiment
beliecaaming

embolden
ferboelde, ferderre

embrace
(n) imaarming, beclip (v)imaarme, beclippe

embroider
duewe needelweurk

embroidery
needelweurk

embroil
muddele, ferwickele

embroilment
muddling, ferwickling

embryo
embryoew, seed

emend
ferbettere, berietige

emendation
ferbettring, berietiging

emerald
(adj) brietgreen (n)emerald, brietgreen

emerge
unfoelde, cueme out (up), shoewe self

emergence
unfoelding, outcueming

emergency
(adj) unfoerseen (n)cwickhappning,
cwickwoew, unfoerseen, helpneed

emergent
unfoeldend, outcuemend, upcuemend

emeritus
emerritus

emery
emmer **emery paper**- emmerpapeer

emetic
(adj) beheevend, beretchend (n)beheevmiddel,
beretchmiddel

emigrant
(hoem)landleever, (hoem)landfersaeker,
landferhouser, emigrant

emigrate
(hoem)landfersaeke, landferhouse emigrerre

emigration
(hoem)landfersaeking, ferhousing, emigraassen

eminence
hiet, loftigness, graetness, (R.C. Church)-
Yor(Hiss) Eminens

eminent
hy, loftig, standend hy, outstandend

emissary
boedberrder, errendberrder

emission
out-, fortsending

emit
sende out (fort), givve off

emollient
(adj) fersoftened, suedend, wiekend (n)
fersoftner, sueder, wieker

emotion
strang feeling, (mind)bewaying, feeling

emotional
fillingsful, besteurend, (mind)bewayend, filled
mid (mind)bewaying, feelingsbesteurend

empanel
swerre in, be listed

emperor
kieser

emphasis
stress, afterdruck, wict, hevvigness, betoening

emphasize
stresse, putte afterdruck (wict), betoene

emphatic
afterdrucklig

empire
kieserdum

empirical
empeerish

employ
hyere, givve weurk (aarbied) tue, brueke

employee
weurker, aarbieder, nuewhyer

employer
weurkgivver, aarbiedgivver

employment
weurk, aarbied

empower
bemiete, becrafte, givve miet tue

empress
kieseress

emptiness
emptigness, (fig) iedelness

empty
(adj) emptig, (fig) iedel (v) emptige

emu
eemuew

emulate
fereevene, strieve after, be liek, duewe liek
(after)

emulation
fereevning, liekdeed

emulsion
emulsen

enable
bemeense

enabling
(adj) bemeensend (gerund) bemeensen

enact
ferordere, ferbeheste

enactment
ferordring, ferbehest

enamel
enamell

enamoured of
in luev mid, ferlueved av

enchant
bewitche, betoubere

enchanting
bewitchend, betoubrend

enchantment
bewitching, betoubring

encircle
besette, imsette

encirclement
besetting, imsetting

enclose
shutte in, penne in, betiene, beclisse

enclosure
inshutter, betiener

encode
incoede

encompass
imsitte, imselle, imgoewe

encore
(interj) agen, biss

encounter
(n) meeting, treffing (v) meete, treffe, runne
intue

encourage
givve haart tue, betrimme, fermuedige,
mudige up, ferboelde

encouraging
behaartnend, ferboeldend, fermuedigend

encroach
goewe beyond, goewe oever, crosse oever

encroachment
oevergang, oevercross

encrust
becruste

encumber
hindere, burdene, loede doun mid

encyclical
ensiclikel, poepletter

encyclopedia
ensiclopeeder

encyclopedic
ensiclopeedish

end
(n) end (v) ende

endanger
bringe in(tue) gefaar

endear
make deer (belueved)

endearing
deermaekend, ferdeerend

endearment
deermaeking, ferdeerness

endeavor
(n) strief (v) strieve

endemic
endemmish

ending
ending

endless
endless, sonder end,
unendlig

endow
begiftige, beshenke, bedeele

endowed
begiftiged, beshenked, bedelt

endowment
begiftiging, beshenking, bedeeling

endurable
lastbaar

endurance
lastbaarness

endure
laste, gebiede, reffene, tolle, **endure
punishment**- berre straff (or bestraffing) av

enduring
lastend, getildig

enema
clister

enemy
(n) feend, foew, unfrend, hettend (adj)
feendlig, foewlig

energetic
ennergish

energy
ennergee, miet

enfeeble
weekene

enfold
wrappe in foelds, foeldwrappe

enforce
ferdwinge, bestrengte, incrafte

enforceable
ferdwingbaar

enforcement
ferdwinging, bestrengt, incraftness

engage
ferbinde, hyere, (gears) - meshe, locke in

engaged
betroeted tue, pledged tue, (gears)- meshed,
locked in, (military) - locked in

engagement
betroeting, pledg, (military)- hild, fiet, kemp,
setch

engender
feroersacke, bringe intue beeing, maeke +
e-infinitive, ferwaeke, waekene

engine
moeter, masheen, locomoetiv

engineer
engineer, masheencrafter

engineering
engineering, masheencraft

England
England

English
(language)- English, (people)-English

Englishman
Englander, Englishman, Englishfrouw

engrave
etche, ingraeve

engraver
etcher, ingraever

engraving
etching, ingraeving

engulf
swalloewe up, oeverwelme

enhance
fergraetere, hictene, fermoere dee weurt av

enhancement
fergraetring, hictning, weurtfermoering

enigma
riddel, enigma

enigmatic
riddlish, enigmatish

enjoin
beherre, ferbidde

enjoy
geneete, **enjoy oneself**- amuserre self

enjoyable
geneetbaar

enjoyment
genot, geneetingen, genuffen

enlarge
fergraete

enlargement
fergraeting

enlighten
ferlietene, bekenne

enlightenment
ferlietning

enlist
inliste in, seeke help av, verb +freewillig

enlistment
inlisting, deentied

enliven
lievene up, believen

enmity
feendship, foewship, unfrendship

ennoble
fereddele

enormity
oeverwickedness

enormous
oevergraet

enough
enuff

enphesema
lungsickness, blacklung

enrich
ferritche, beguede

enriching
ferritchend

enrichment
ferritchness, begudness

enroll
wriete in, inliste, (univ) - matriculerre

enrollment
inwrieting, inlist

enshrine
inshriene

enshroud
shroude oever

ensign
badg, toeken, flag, (naval officer)-
understedhoelder

enslave
beslaeve

ensnare
besnerre, begriene

ensue
folge, folloewe

ensuing
folgend

entangle
maeke tangeled, besnerre, (becueme, be)
tangeled (up), betangele

enter
goewe in, cueme in, betredde

enterprise
undertaeking, undernieming

enterprising
underniemend

entertain
fermaeke, underhoelde, amuserre

entertaining
fermaekend, underhoeldend

entertainment
fermaeking, underhoelding

enthrone
introene

entire
hoel, fullcuemen, anlang, fullswied

entirely
hoellig, fullig, anlang, fullswied

enthusiasm
iever

enthusiastic
iefrig

entice
lurre, ferleede, costene

enticement
lur, costning

entitle to
berietige tue

entitlement
berietiging

entity
wiet, being, waesen

entomb
burree, begraeve

entomologist
insectcrafter, entomoloeg

entomology
entomoloegee, insectcraft

entrails
innerdeels

entrance
(building)-inway, ingang (freeway)- onway

entrap
betrappe

entrapment
betrapping

entrench
digge in

entrenched
dug in

entrust
fertruste mid (tue), fertrouwe in

entry
(building) inway, ingang

entwine
betwiene, betwiste

enumerate
telle, naeme oen by (after) oen, liste

enumeration
listing

enunciate
saye out cleerlig, putte fort

envelope
(n)imslaag, wrapper papeerhoeld(er), cuverrt
(v) foelde in (up), wrappe up, hiede

envious
niedish, befestig, befestful

environment
imgivving, imweld

environmental
imweldish

environs
imreech

envy
(n) nied, befestfulness (v) beniede, befeste

enzyme
ensiem

ephemeral
unlastend, fleetend, shorttiedig

epic
(adj) heldtaelish, eppish (n) heldtael, eppic,
helddiet, saaga

epicenter
middelpunt, midpunt

epicure
fuedcrafter

epidemic
(adj) epidemmish, wiedspred (n) epidemmic

epidermis
outerskin

epilepsy
shaeksickness, epilepsee

epilepic
(adj) epileptish (n) epileptiker

epilog(ue)
afterweurd, epiloeg

Epiphany
Epifaan

episcopacy
bisshophud

episcopal
bisshopish

episode
episoed

epistle
apostelletter

epitaph
graevwrit, epitaaf

epithet
benaeming

epitome
ferliecaaming, inboediging, epitoem

epitomize
havve(shoewe, be) dee liecaaming av

epoch
tiedperrk

equal
(adj) eeven, beliek (n) eevner, belieker (v)
fereevene, eevene up

equality
eevenness, beliekness

equalize
fereevene, eevene up

equanimity
mindeevenness

equate
fereevene, maeke eeven, maeke beliek

equation
fereevning, belieking

equator
aecwaator, eevenfaarness

equatorial
aecwaatorish

equestrian
(adj)horslig (n) horsrieder

equidistant
eevenfaar

equilateral
eevensied(s)

equilibrium
eevenwiet

equinox
eevenniet

equip
ecwippe, betuele, begerre

equipment
ecwipping, tuels, begerring

equitable
ferr

equity
ferrness

equivalent
(adj)eeven, beliek (n)eevner, belieker

equivocal
tweemeenig, hedgig, misleedend, tweesensig

equivocate
misleede, hedge, begraage, speeke mid
twinmeening (tweesens)

era
yeertelling

erase
wiepe out (av), rubbe out, scraepe av

eraser
outwieper, outrubber, scraeper

erasure
outwieping, outrubbing

ere
(poet.) err

erect
(adj)upriet, stiff (v) sette(putte) up, raese,
putte tuegedder (saamel)

ermine
herrmelin

erode
werre away, rotte, weursene, eete away at

erosion
werringaway, rotting, weursning

erotic
eroetish

erotica
eroetiker

eroticism
eroetishness

err
be wrang (mistaeken), duewe wrang, misduewe, falle intue mistaekenness

errand
errend, boed

erratic
twistend, wandrend

erroneous
mistaeken, wrang, faltig

error
mistaek, falt, misdeed, gedoel

erupt
burste fort (out), braeke out

eruption
outburst, outbraek

escalator
rollend sterrway

escape
(n) getaway, braekeout, braekfree, fliet, ferleeving (v) gette away(free), ferleeve, unyelde, flee, braeke lues (out) (free)

escort
(n) beleeder, escort (v) beleede, escorterre

esoteric
hiemlig. esoterrish

especial
= **special**

espionage
spying, spionaag

essay
(n) pruef, ferseek, ferhandling, wrieting (v) ferseeke, proberre

essence
wessen, essens, paarfuem

essential
wessentlig, wietig

establish
besette, sette up, befaste, upreere, bestaade

establishment
upreering,besetting, **the Establishment**- dee Miethoelderhud

estate
oewendum, oewenship, landhoeldings,besit, rank **real estate**- landhoeldings

esteem
(n)acting, hy weurt (v)acte, hoeld hy, hoelde s.o. tue be weurtig, beweurte

estimate
(n) bereckning, tellinggess, berieming (v) bereckene, gesse dee telling, berieme

estrange
ferfremde

estrangement
ferfremding

estrogen
estrogen

estuary
inlet, seeaarm

et cetera
e.a. (en anders), e.s.f. (en so fort)

etch
etche

etching
etching

eternal
forevver, elderlang, alltied, unendig

eternity
forevverness, alltiedness, unendigness

ether
eeter

ethical
ettish

ethics
ettiker

Ethiopia
Etioep

Ethiopian
(adj) Etioepish (n) Etioeper

ethnic
etnish, av folkgrueps

ethnography
folkcultur, folkways, etnograaf

ethnology
folkwayscraft, etnoloegee

etiquette
etiket

etymological
etimoloegish

etymology
etimoloegee

eucharist
housel

eulogize
loffe

eulogy
loff, hyloff

eunuch
gelded, eenuc

euphemism
softweurd, softweurding

Europe
Eerop

European
(adj) Eeropish (n)Eeroper

evacuate
leeve, widdraawe, feremptige, pulle out

evacuation
leeving, feremptiging, widdraawing, pullout

evacuee
feremptiged

evade
shunne, imgoewe

evaluate
beweurte

evaluation
beweurting, shatting

evangelical
evangaelish

evangelist
evangaeliker

evangelize
becristene, preeche dee gospel

evaporate
fersteeme, steeme away

evaporation
fersteeming, waysteeming

evasion
shunning , imgang

eve
eev

even
eeven

evening
eevning, eeven

evenly
eevenlig

evenness
eevenness

event
happning, befalling, betieding (sports)-widplay

eventful
happningful, betiedingful

eventide
eeventied

eventual
endlig

ever
evver

every
eefrig

everybody
all, aller, eefriger

everyday
alldays

everyone
all, aller, eefriger

everything
aller, all tings

evident
cleer, sweedel, geseem, maarkbaar, oepenbaar

evil
(adj) eevil, bad (n) evil, foeken **the Evil One**-
dee Boes (vil), dee Eevil Oen

evince
shoewe, maeke cleer

evoke
calle fort, drauwe out

evolution
evoluessen, unfoelding, unwinding

evolutionist
evoluessner

evolve
evolve, unfoelde, unwinde, sette free, givve av,
bewaye, becueme bekent

ewe
uew, muedersheep

exacerbate
fershaarpere, weursene, maeke shaarper
(weurs)

exact
(adj) genouw, presies, utter, saem, bissen,
fertiet, stipt (v)fordere

exacting
fordrend

exactness
genouwigness, fertietness

exaggerate
oeverdrieve, oeversaye, oeverduewe, goewe
beyond

exaggeration
oeverdrieving, oeversaying

exalt
raese, loffe, fille mid (bliss, pried, etc.), hictene

exam
= **examination**

examination
underseeking, ferheering,
test, geshee, beseeing

examine
lucke at (intue, oever), teste, underseeke,
ferheere, besee

example
foerbild, muster

excavate
holloewe out, digge out, maeke aan holloew
(hoel), ferholloewe

excavation
ferholloewing

exceed
goewe beyond, be beyond, be graeter (moer)
daan

excel
oevertreffe, ferbeste, stande out, oevermeete

excellent
betungen, best, outstandend

except (for)
(prep) outtaeken, outen (v)sondere out

excepting
(prep) outsondert

exception
outsondring

exceptional
oever, bissen gud, besonder

exerpt
pullout, cutout

excess
oeverness, oevermutch

excessive
oefrig, oevermutch

exchange
(n) ferwissling (v) ferwissele

exchequer
landhoerd

excise
(n) bruektax (v)cutte out, sniede out

excitable
steurbent

excite
steure,besteure, calle fort, lifte dee feelings av,
winde up, trille

excited
besteured ,upwund, trilled

excitement
hy feelings, steurings, wundupness

exciting
steurend, feelingliftend, trillend

exclaim
shoute, ruepe out

exclamation
shout, outruep

exclamatory
outruepend

exclude
sliete out, baare

exclusion
outslieting, baaring

exclusive
(adj) outslietend, aloen, oenig (n)exclusiv

excommunicate
(rel) excomunikerre, benieme oen av
membership

excommunication
(rel) excomuni- caassen, membershiploss

excrement
outsifting

excrete
sifte out

exculpate
ferungiltige, ferunshuldige

exculpation
ferungiltiging, ferunshuldiging

exculpatory
ferungiltigend, ferunshuldigend

excursion
siedtrip, (mil.) oeverfall

excusable
oeverluckbaar, (fer)ungiltbaar, (fer)
unshuldbaar

excuse
(n) (fer)ungiltiging, (fer)unshuldiging
(pretext)-fals fercleering (v) (fer)ungiltige, (fer)
unshuldige, free av

execute
(law) cwelle, kille by laaw, (carry out)
fullbringe, berre out

execution
(law) cwelling, (carrying out) fullbringing

executioner
(law) cweller

executive
(adj) laawmaekend (n) (com) bedrifthandler,
companeehed , steerder

executor
willoutberrder

exemplary
foerbildig

exempt
(adj) freed, unbund (n) free, unbinde

exemption
freedum, unbinding

exercise
(n) uefning, bewaying (v) uevene, begoewe,
duewe bewayings, bewaye self

exert
sette self tue, spanne in self, laye on

exertion
inspanning, onlaying

exhale
breete out

exhaust
(n)luesning (v) sette free, luesene, ferbrueke,
lette goewe, draene

exhausted
ferbrueked, draened, (oever)tyered, weerig

exhaustion
(oever)tyeredness, weerigness

exhaustive
(complete) turroew, allintaekend, oeverall

exhibit
(n) shoewstuek (v) shoewe, laye out

exhibition
shoewing, outlaying

exhort
begge, beseeche

exhumation
digup, unerrting

exhume
digge up, unerrte

exile
(n) ferbanning, bannishing (v) ferbanne, bannishe

exist
livve bestand, bestande, livve, wesse

existence
bestand

existent
bestanden, livvend

exit
(n)(building, park, etc.) - outway, outgang (freeway) offway (v) leeve by, goewe(cueme) out, goewe av, outwaye

exodus
outwaandring, **Exodus**- Exodus

exonerate
unbinde, free av gilt (shuld)

exorbitant
beyondish, oeverhy

exorcise
drieve eout, beswerre

exorcism
(goest)beswerring

exorcist
(goest)beswerrder

exotic
fremdlandish, exoetish, nit inborn, elteedish

expand
spredde out, broedene, stretche out, unfoelde wiedene

expanse
graet bredt (widt), broedlands

expansion
outspredding(-broedning)

expatriate
ferbanne, leeve
oens land

expect
foerwaache, lucke foerway tue, lucke tue, hoepe tue

expectancy
foerwaach

expectant
foerwa

expedience
selfintrest (-behuef), endmeens, meens tue aan end

expediency
= **expedience**

expedient
goelreechend, endbringend

expedite
ferhaeste, speede up

expedition
huntingtrip, haest,
speed, cwickness

expeditious
fast, cwick,
speedy, snell

expel
drieve out, ferdrieve,
feryaage

expend
ferbrueke, spende

expendable
ferbruekbaar

expenditure
ferbruek, spending

expense
cost, outbetalling,
outlay

expensive
costlig, hybetallig

experience
(n) errfaaring, undergang, foerdeed (v) errfaare, undergoewe, livve true, gebiede

experiment
(n) pruefnieming, ferseek, experriment (v) nieme pruefs, ferseeke, experrimenterre

experimental
pruefniemig

expert
(adj) skilled, craftig (n) skillder, crafter

expiration
outbreeting, end, endcueming, endreeching, det

expire
cueme tue aan end, reeche aan end, ende. dye

explain
fercleere, maeke cleer, givve dee meening av, telle wy

explanation
fercleering

explanatory
fercleerend

expletive
oet, filler

explicable
fercleerbaar

explicit
cleer, outspoeken

explode
bloewe up, exploderre, burste, braeke fort

exploit
(n) boeld deed, heldendeed, (v) maeke bruek av, taeke foerhelp av, misbrueke

exploration
underseeking

exploratory
underseekings-(combining form, e.g., underseekingsweurk)

explore
underseeke, ferfinde

explorer
underseeker, ferrder

explosion
bloewup, outbraek, burst, exploesen

explosive
(adj) burstish, bloewuppish, exploedish (n) burststuff, exploesiv

exponent
fertalker, pusher, (math) expoenent, fermennigfoelder

export
(n) outsending, export (v) sende out, exporterre

exporter
outsender, exporter

exporting
outsending, exporting

expose
sette out. laye berr (oepen), shoewe fort, belietene, /maeke bekent

expose
undecking

exposure
outsetting, berrlaying, oepenlaying, belietning

expound
sette fort, fercleere, beretche

express
(adj) cleer, spoeken (n) (speed-) snelltraen. speedsend, swiftsend, fastsend (v) speeke, saye out, maeke bekent

expression
sayway, feelingshoewing, feelingluck

expressive
feelingful, meeningful

express-way
(speed-. swift-) fastway

expropriate
unoewne, unbeseeme, unbemeete

expulsion
ferdrieving

expunge
(taeke-) nieme out, wiepe out

expurgate
clense

expurgation
clensing extant (still) bestandend

extemporaneous
offhandlig

extemporize
duewe offhand

extend
ferlenge, lengtene, wiedene. broedene, stretche, reeche

extension
ferlenging, wiedning, broedning

extensive
broed, wied, faarreechend

extent
lengt, bredt, widt, reech, imfang

extenuate
fermilde, lessene

extenuating
lessnend, fermildend

exterior
(adj) outer, outsied - (combining form), outermoest (n)outsied, (fig.) outerluck

exterminate
duewe away mid, fernitte, wiepe out

extermination
fernitting, wiepout

exterminator
fernitter, outwieper

external
(adj) outer, outsied (combining form) (n. pl.)
externals- outerlucks

extinct
ded, unlivvend, outgestaarven

extinction
undergang

extinguish
fernitte, putte out, smuedere, cwelle

extinguisher
fyercweller

extol
ferheffe, hyloffe

extort
offpresse, twiste out

extortion
offpressing

extra
(adj/n) extra, sperr,
oever

extract
(n) pullout, extract (v) pulle out, pulle

extraction
tandpulling

extradite
(hande)turne oever

extradition
(handing-) turningoever

extraneous
fremd, unsifted

extraordinary
unbewoenlig, ungemaen

extraterrestrial
(adj) unerrtlig (n)unerrter

extravagance
oeverdeed, oeverspending

extravagant
oeverduen, oevercostlig, oevershoewig

extravaganza
oevershoew

extreme
(adj/n) furdest, outermoest, utmoest

extremist
furdestgoewer, utmoestgoewer

extremity
outermoest, utmoest, liecaamlim, hands en feet

extricate
sette free, befree, free, luesene

extrinsic
fremd, mislinked

extrovert
extrovert

exude
uese, seepe, leeke, drippe, swette

exult
yuebele, ferblisse

exultation
yuebling, ferbliss

eye
ieger

eyebrow
iegerbrouw

eyelid
iegerlid

eyesight
iegersiet

eyestrain
iegerweerigness

f

fable
faabel, mit, oeldtael, lessentael,saaga

fabric
stuff, web, webbing, weeving

fabricate
maeke up, tinke up, lye, fabrikerre, maeke,
bouwe

fabrication
ly, untruet, fabricaassen

fabricator
fabrikerrder

fabulist
faabler,
faabeldieter

fabulous
faablig, taatbildig, unbeleevbaar, astundend,
wunderful

facade
bildingfoersied, bouwenfoersied

face
(n) ansiet, foersied, **lose face**- luese selfweurt
save face- redde selfweurt (v) stande befoer
face up to- daye out

faceless
ansietless

facelift
ansietfersheening

facet
faset

facetious
unerrnest, unerrnst

facial
(adj) ansiet-(combining form) (n)
ansietbehandling

facile
floewend, reddig, shalloew

facilitate
maeke lieter (eeder), ferlietere, fereedere

facility
skill, unaarfedness, meens, ferlietersted

facing
fercladding, besaats

facsimile
copee, liekness

fact
deed, weurkligness, truet

faction
innercamphud, splittergruep, innercamp

factious
innercampbringend, besplittend

factitious
cunstlig

factor
factor

factory
-weurks, fabreek

faculty
teecherhud, fermayenness, craft, mindskill

133

fad
fad, craes

fade
widdere, wilte, ferwelke, (colors) ferlietere, lietene

fag
fag

fail
1. falle short 2. weekene, dye away 3. stoppe weurkene 4. flunke, mislucke 5. goewe bankrupt 6. unbelinge, fersaye 7. misfolge (-folloewe)

failing
unbelinging, misluck, falt, weekness

failure
(person) misfolger, fersayer, shortfall (thing) misdeed, misfolging

faint
(adj) week, dim, sliet (n) swuen (v) swuene, falle intue aan swuen

faint-hearted
weekhaarted, unmuedig

fane
faen, gladlig, willendlig

fair-1
ferr(beautiful, cleen, liet, just, promising, average)

fairness -1
ferrness

fair-2
yeermaarket, caarneval, fest, foelkfest

fairly-1
ferrlig

fairway
ferrway

fairy
fay

fairyland
fayland

fairytale
faytael

faith
fertrouwen, trouw, beleef, stedfastness

faith-based
trouwgrunded, trouwtied

faithful
trouw, upriet, oerlig, stedfast

faithless
trouwless

fake
(adj/n) faek

falcon
falk

fall
(n) fall, (season of the year) fall, haarvest(tied) (v) falle

fall away
(n) fall(ing)away (v) falle away

fall back
(n) fallback (v) falle back

fall down
(n) dounfall (v) falle doun

fall in
falle in

fall off
(n) falloff (v) falle av

fall out
(n) fallout, fallingout (v) falle out

fall over
falle oever

fall through
(n) falltrue (v) falle true

fallacious
misleedend, fals, mistaeken

fallacy
mistaek. gedoel, untruet

fallibility
mistaekbaarness

fallible
mistaekbaar

fallow
falloew

fallow-deer
falloewherrt

false
fals, mistaeken

falsehood
falshud, ly, untruet

falsification
ferfalsing

falsify
ferfalse

falsity
falsness, falshud, mistaek, ly

falsetto
falset, falsetstem

falter
(n) falter (v) faltere

fame
ruem, wellbekentness

famed
beruemd

familiar
gemaen(-sum) fertrouwd, bekent, familiaar

familiarity
fertrouwdness, familiaaarness

familiarize
maeke(self) fertrouwd
mid

family
famillee, houshoeld, kindred. kin

famine
hungersneed,
fuedlack

famish
(vt) hungere out (vi) ferhungere

famous
beruemd, wellbekent

fan
(blower) luftbloewer, bloewer, ventilator
(aficionado) folger, iefriger, ellenwueder

fanatic
(adj) fanaatish (n) fanaatiker

fanaticism
fanaatishness

fancier
skillder,crafter

fancy
(adj) hy (prices), skillful, gud(quality), bedecked (n) lieking, wim. mindbild, wimsee
(v) see(imagine), havve aan lieking for, ferbilde
self

fanfare
huepla, outshoewing, bussel

fang
fang, fangtand

fantastic
fantaastish

fantasy
fantasee

far
faar **the Far East**- dee Faar Eest

fare
(n) ferr, cost, ressgeld, fued (v) ferre, resse,
cueme out, eete, be givven fued

farewell
(adj) ferrwell (n) ferrwell (intj) ferrwell

far-fetched
faarfetched

far-flung
faarflung

farm
(n) tillsted, faarm (v) tille, landtille, faarme

farrow
(n) farroew (v) farroewe

far-seeing
faarseeyend

far-sighted
faarsieted

farther
faarder

farthermost
faardermoest

farthest
faardest

farthing
faarding

fascinate
bewitche, beheede, hoelde dee heed av,
fassinerre

fascinating
bewitchend, beheedend, fassinerrend

fascination
bewitchendness, beheedendness, fassinaassen

fascism
fashissing

fascist
(n) fashist (adj) fashistish

fashion
(n) moed, maek, form, shaep, way (v) maeke,
forme, shaepe

fast-1
(adj) fast, speedig, swift, cwick, snell

fast-2
(n) fast (v) faste

fasten
fassene, maeke fast, linke

fastener
fassner, huck

fastness
fastness

fat
(n) fat (adj) fat, tick

fatal
dedlig, ferdedlig

fatalism
fatalling

fatality
detmishap, detunfall

fate
lot, duem

fated
foerbestemmed, foerduemed

father
faader

fatherhood
faaderhud

fatherless
faaderless

fatherly
faaderlig

fathom
faademe

fatigue
(n) weerigness, tyerdness (v) becueme weerig,
tyere

fatten
fattene, maeke fat,
becueme fat

fatty
(adj) fattig (n) fattig

fatuous
sillig

faucet
tap, waatertap

fault
(n) falt, shuld, flaaw, defect, misdeed, mistaek,
shortcueming (v) falte, finde falt mid

faultless
faltless, flaawless, faltfree

faulty
faltig, flaa
wed

favor
(n) kinddeed, kindness, guddeed,gudness,
gunst, gudwill (v) begunstige, givve gunst
tue, shoewe lieking for, lucke liek

favorable
gunstig, (weather)-
geneetbaar, mild

favored
begunstiged

favorite
(adj/n) bestlieked, belueved (n) gunstling

favoritism
bestliekness

fawn-1
yeerling, roewcalf

fawn-2
fonne

fear
(n) feer, angst (v) feere, havve feer av

fearful
feerful

-fearing
-feerend (e.g., **godfearing** -godfeerend)

fearless
feerless

feasibility
duewbaarness

feasible
duewbaar, lieklig

feast
(n) feest, gebeerschip (v) feeste

feat
deed, hydeed, wunderdeed

feather
fedder

feature
(adj) foermoest, maen (n) maek, form, shaep, lucks, standout, maendraaw (v) maeke foermoest, fermaene

February
Februaar

federal
(adj) ferbond-(combining form), ferbonden, faederall

fee
fee

feeble
week, swack

feed
(n) feed (v) feede

feel
(n) feel (v) feele

feeling
feeling

feign
faeke, misleede, ferplaye

feint
seembewaying, shaam

feldspar
feldspaar

fell-1
did falle

fell-2
(n) fell (v) felle

fell-3
(adj) haaruewgrim, grim

fell-4
(animal hide) fell

fell-5
fell, muer, doun

fellow
(adj) felloew (n) felloew

felon
wrangduewer, criminell

felonious
wrangdeedig

felony
wrangdeed, hymisdeed, capitallferbraeken

felt-1
did feel, (pp) felt

felt-2
felt

female
(adj) frouwlig, wieflig, shee- (combining form) (n) she

female line
frouwkin,
wiefkin

female sex
frouwhud,
wiefhud

feminine
frouwlig

femininity
frouwligness

femur
tyboen

fen
fen, swamp, maarsh, moraas

fence
(n) shelding, inshutting, hoeldback (v) shutte in, installe
inshutting, (sport)-fensing

fencer
fenser

fencing
inshutting, fensing

fend off
turne asied, keep away (off)

fennel
fennel

feral
untaemed, wild

fer-de-lance
ferrdelaans

ferment
yiste

fermentation
yisting

fern
ferrn

ferocious
haaruewgrim, meen, wild

ferocity
haaruewgrimness, meenness, wildness

Ferris wheel
Ferrisweel

ferro-
iesen-

ferry
(n) ferree(boet) (v) ferree

fertile
fruetbaar, beloemig, wastembaar, ritch

fertility
fruetbaarness

fertilize
beseede

fertilizer
beseeeding

ferule
rod

fervent
hot, burnend, gloewend, errnest, fyrig, wilmig

fervor
graet heet, fyer, iever, wilm

fester
(n) pussing, puss-soer (v) fertorne, ferbittere, etterne, pusse

festival
festday, festivall, fest

festive
festlig, festivity
festligness

fetch
fetche

fetid
stinkend, smellig

fetter
(n) fetter (v) fettere

feud
(n) ongoewend fiet, clanfiet (v) clanfiete, fiete

ferver
feever

feverish
feevrish(Pronouce: feev rish.)

few
(adj/prn) fuew

fiance(e)
(both sexes) betroeted, belueved

fiasco
fiascoew

fib
(n) wietly (v) telle wietlies

fiber
treds, faesel

fibrous
treddish, faeslig

fickle
fickel

fiction
maedup tales, untruet

fictional
= fictitious

fictitious
maedup, untruew

fiddle
(n) fiddel (v) fiddele

fidelity
trouw

fidget
fidgete

field
feld

fiend
feend

fiendish
feendish

fierce
haaruewgrim, wild, heftig

fiery
fyrig (Missing section)

fortnight
fuerniet

fortress
fasting, stranghoeld, fort

fortuitous
tuefallig

fortunate
lucklig

fortune
luck, tuefall

fortune-teller
lieffoerteller, suetsayer, truetsayer

forty
fuertig

forum
forum

forward
foerway

fossil
fossil

foster
(adj) foster (v) fostere

foster child
fosterchild

foster parents
fosterelders

foul
(adj) foul (n) foul (v) foule

foulness
foulness

foul up
foule up, befoule

found-1
(pt.-pp of **finde**) fund

found-2
sette up, befaste

found-3
caste

foundation
befasting, grunds, staddel

founder-2
befaster

founder-3
caster

foundling
fundling

fount
= **fountain**

fountain
well, spring, ord, drinkwell

fountain head
springstreem, ord

fountain pen
fillpen, inkpen

four
fuer

fourfold
fuerfoeld

fourscore
fuerscoer

foursome
fuersum, fuerset

foursquare
fuersieded, rietwinklig, unyeldend, frank, fortriet(-lig)

fourteen
fuerteen

fourteenth
fuerteent

fourth
fuert

fowl
foul, foegel

fox
faax

foxy
faaxig

fracas
brall

fraction
braek, underdeel

fracture
(n) braek (v) braeke

fragile
braekbaar

fragility
braekbaarness

fragment
braekbit, braekstuek

fragmentary
braekbittig, in bits

fragrance
sweetsmell, duft

fragrant
sweetsmellig, duftig

frail
braekbaar, swack

frailty
braekbaarness, swackness

frame
(n) fraem (v) fraeme

framework
fraemweurk

France
Frankland

franchise
bedriftriet, sellriet, riet, stemriet

frank
frank

frankly
franklig

Frank
Frank

frankincense
weeroek

frantic
angerwild, tornwild, smaartswild, sorgenwild

fraternal
bruederlig

fraternity
bruedership, (-hud), bruederligness, liektinkerhud, bruedershiphous

fraternization
ferbruedring

fraternize
ferbruedere self
mid

fratricide
bruedermurder, siblingmurder, landsmanmurder

fraud
beswieking, swindel. bedraag

fraudulent
beswiekingful, bedraaglig

fraught
fraat (mid), full (av)

fray-1
brall

frayed-2
worn, ragged

frazzled
= frayed

freak
freek

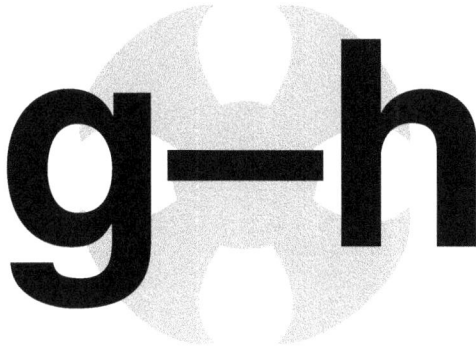

g–h

Ghost
goest

Ghostwriter
goestwryster

Godchildren
godkinder

Gristmill
gristmill

Groundball
grunder

Gest
guest
Gestfrendlig
Gestfrendligness

Handrail
handreil

Harvest moon
Haarvestmeun

Hayday
heyday, besttyd

Host
gestherr
Hostess
gestfrouw

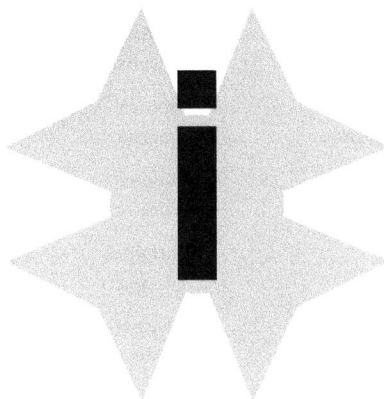

i

I
ic

ice
ys

Iceland
Ysland

ichthyology
fishcraft, ictioloegie

icicle
ysickel

icing
ysing, frosting

iconography
iconograafie

icy
ysig

idea
idea, taatgift

ideal
ideaal

idealistic
idealistish

idealize
idealiserre

identical
identish

identification
identifiserring

identify
identifiserre

identity
identiteit

ideology
ideoloegie

idiocy
idioetness

idiom
idioem

idiomatic
idiomaatic

idiot
idioet

idiotic
idioetish

idle
(adj) ydel, nitsduewend (v) ydele

idol
ofgod, idoel

idolatrous
ofgoddish, idoelatrish

idoltry
ferofgodding, idoelatrie

idolize
ferofgodde, idoliserre

if
if

igneous
kindlish

ignitable
ferkindelbaar

ignite
ferkindele, sette aan fyer, ferbrande

ignition
ferkindling; (auto) unstecking

ignoble

uneidel,

unaadel

ignoramus
nitwitter, dumhed

ignorance
unwittenness

ignorant
unwittend, unkundig

ignore
ignorerre, nit beacte

iguana

igwaana

ill
il, sic

Iliad
Iliaad

ill-advised
unferstandig, ilberaaded

ill-behaved
ill-behavd, unmannerlig

illegal
unlaawful, unwetting

illegality
unlaawfulness, unwettigness

illegible
unriedbaar, unleisbaar

illegitimacy
unlawfulness, unwettigness

illegitimate
unlawful, unwettig

ill-fated
ungeluckig

illicit
See illegal

illiteracy
ungeletterdness, unlerrnedness

ill-luck
ungeluc

illness
ilness, sicness

illogical
illoegish

ill-treat
mishandele

illuminate
ferlyte, lyte up

illumination
ferlyting

ill-use
mishandel

illusion
illuesen, mislieder

illusive
unfangbaar

illustrate
illustrerre

illustration
illustrerring, illustraasen

illustrious
beruemt, welwitten

ill will
ilwil, ilwilligness

image
beld, ofbelding

imagery

ferbelding, foerstelling

immigrant

inwanderder, immigrant

immigrate
inwandere, immigrerre

immigration
inwandring, immigraasen

imminent
driegend, at hand, **be-** befoerstande unmittel-
baar

imaginable
tinkbaar

imaginary
tinkbelding

imagination
ferbelding, foerstelling

imaginative
ritch aan ferbelding

imagine

ferbeld (self),
foerstelle (self)

imbecile
imbesil, idioet, dumhed

imitable

lykduebaar

imitate

lykduewe (after-),
immiterre

imitation
afterdied, immitaasen

imitative
afterduewend

imitator
lykduewer (after-)

immaculate
smutless; (rel.) beflect

immaterial
unferskillig

immature
unryp, grien

immaturity
unrypness

immeasurable
unmetbaar

immediate
fernouwig, sofortig, (location) nierest;
daadelig, rytnouw

immerse
dippe in, underdippe

immersion
underdipping

immobile
unbeweybaar

immobility
unbeweybaarness

immobilize
immobiliserre

immodest
unbeshyden

immolation
offer

immoral
unmoraalish, unrytig

immorality
immoraliteit

immortal
(adj/n) undyig, undybaar

immovable
unbeweybaar

immune
immuen

immunity
immuniteit

immunize
meike immuen

immutable
unferanderbaar

impair
ferlessene, ferwiekene

impala
impaala

impartial
ferr, unpartydig

impartiality
ferrness, unpartydigness

impassable
unpaserrbaar, unbegaanbaar

impasse
impas

impassive
unbeweylig, unferstoerbaar

impatience
ungeduld

impatient
ungeduldig

impeach
claage aan

impeccable
faltless, flaawless

impede
ferhindere, belette

impediment
ferhindring, beletsel

impel
dryve aan (fort)

impending
overhanging, upcuemend

impenetrable
undurdringbaar

impenitent
unatynig, ferstoct

imperative
bedraggled, mustig, notwendig; (gram)
imperrativ

imperceptible
unmaarkbaar

imperfect
flaawd, unfulcuemen, imperrfect

imperfection
unfulcuemenness, gebrec

imperial
kyserlig

imperial
bringe in gefaar

impermanent
unnbestendig, unlanglastend

impermeable
undurdringbaar

impermissible
ungetaavbaar, unferletbaar

impersonable
unpersoenlig

impersonate
ferpersoenlige

impersonation
ferpersoenliging

impetus
fortness, dryvmyt, fortweyness

implement
(work) tuel, geret

implant
(n) implant (v) implante

implicate
betrecke in, inwickele

implication
inwickling

implicit
unbedingt, begreppen

implied
ferhinted

implore
bidde, smecken, begge

imply
ferhinted, underferstud

impolite
unhoflig

import
(n) import, teike-in (v) importerre, teike in

importance
gewict, hevvigness

important
wictig, hevvig

impose
leye up

imposition
upleying

impossibility
unmeyligness

impostor
bedrieger

impotence
unmyt, mytlessness (medical) impotenz

impotent
unmytig, mytless, (med) impotent

impregnable
unnymbaar

impregnate
beswangere

impregnation
befrueting

impresario
impresaariow

impress
indrucke, impresse

impression
indruc, impressen

impressive
indrucweikend, impressiv

imprint
drucken, stempel

imprison
putte (sette) in gefangness

improbability
untrruetsiemlig ness, unlyklihued

improbable
untruetsiemlig, unlyklig

improper
unbeherrlig, betaamlig, unbetaamlig

improve
ferbettere

improvise
improviserre

imprudent
unfoersytig, unclevver, unwys

impulse
impuls

impulsive
impulsiv

impunity
straflessness, straffriedum, straflac

impure
foul, smuttig

impurity
foulness, smuttigness

in
(prep/adv/particle) in ingelocken

inability
unfermeyenness, unbecwaamness

inaccessible
untueganglig

inaccurate
ungenouw

inactive
unwurksum, unbedryvig

inactivity
unwurksumness, unbedryvigness

inadequate
unfulduen

inadmissable
uninletbaar, untueletbaar

inalienable
unbenymbaar

inanimate
unlivvend, unbelift

inaudible
unhierbaar

inauguration
inwyding, instalaasen

in-between
tussenpersoen, inbetwiener

incalculable
unbereckenbaar

incandescent
gloewend, wythot

incapable
unbecwaam

incarnation
incarnaasen, infleshing

incautious
unfoersytig, kerrless

incendiary
(bomb) brandbom, fyerbom

incenz-1
(rel) wiesmoek

incense- 2
(v) fertorne

incentive
aanspurring, forweypush

inch
(n) inch (v) inche

incident
foerfal, insident

incidental(ly)
tuefallig

incision
insnyding, incutting

incite
spurre aan, ferboelde, arouse

incitement
aanspurring

inclement
ruf, haarsh

inclination
liening, sloep, slant

incline
(n) sloep, slant (v) sloepe, slante

include
locke in, shutte in

including
ingelocken

inclusive
ingelocken, incluesiv

incoherent
unferstandlig

incombustible
unbrandbaar, unfyerbaar

income
incuem, incuemen

income tax
incuemtax(-cs), incuemenbelasting

incomparable
unferlykbaar, unlykenbaar

incompetent
kennislackend, witshiplackend

incomplete
unfulcuemend, unfulstandig

incomprehensible
unferstandlig

incongruous
unferynigbaar

inconsequent
inconsicwensiaal

inconsiderate
taatless, bacsytless

inconceivable
untinkbaar

inconstant
feranderlig

incontestable
unbetwistbaar

inch
(n) inch (v) inche

inconvenient
boddersum, gunstlig

inconsistent
unferynigbaar

incorrect
unrytig, incorect

incorrigible
unferbetterlig, unferbetterbaar

increase
(n) fermoering, groewt, tuenyming (v)
fermoere, groewe, tuenyme incredible
unbelievbaar

incriminate
beshuldige begiltige

incurable
unhielbaar

incubate
hatche

indebted
beshuldigd

indecent
unbetaamlig

indecisive
unbesluetless

indeed
indied

indefensible
unbetetchbaar, unbededdigbaar

indelible
unweynymbar, unweywashbaar

independence
selfstandendness

independent
unaanhangend, selfstandend

indescribable
unbewrytbaar, unbescryblig

indestructable
unterrfalbaar, unferduewbaar

indeterminate
unbestimmt

index
index (-cs), wyser; wysfinger

India
Indie

Indian (American)
Indiaaner (m/f)

indicate
shoewe

indication
shoewing

indicative
(gram) indicativ

indicator
(auto) blinker; shoewer

indictment
beshuldiging

indifferent
unfershillig

indigenous
inborn, hierborn

indigent
aarm, behueftig

indigestion
undigestbaarness

indiscreet
unbeshyden

indispensable
unmisbaar, unentberrlig

indisputable
unbetwistbaar

indistinct
unclier, undydelig

individual
(adj) individu'el (n) yner, persoen

indivisible
undielbaar

Indonesia
Indoniesie

Indonesian
(person) Indonieser (language) Indoniesish

indoor
(adj) indoer

indoors
(adv) indoers, outsyd

induce
liede aan, bringe aan'

indulge
givve in tue

indulgent
ingivvend

industrial
industrieel

industrious
wurksum, yfrig

industry
industrie

ineffective
unwurksum

inefficient
unbruekbaar, ungoelriechend

inequality
unbelykness, unievenness

inevitable
unfermydelig

inexcusable
unfergivvig

inexhaustible
unfernittigbaar

inexpensive
guedcuep

inexperienced
unerrfaaren

inexplicable
unferclierbaar

infallible
unfeilbaar

infamous
errless

infamy
shand, errlessness

infancy
nuewborntyd, litlingtyd, kinthued

infant
nuewborn, kint, litling

infantile paralysis
kinderferleiming

infantry
infantrie

infect
befoule, infiserre

infected
befould, infiserrt

infection
befoulness, infecsen

infer
hinte, besluete

inference
hint, beslueting

inferior
minder, minderwurdig, inferioer

inferiority
minderwurdigness

inferior complex
minderwurdignesscomplex (-cs)

infernal
hellish, av hel

inferno
hel

infertile
berren; (egg) unbesieded; unfruetbaar

infest
oeverrunne (cralle) mid, bie parasittish in
(aan)

infested with
befangd mid

infidel
(adj) unbelievig, swey, (n) unbeliever

infidelity
untrouw

infield
infeld (baseball)

infielder
infelder (baseball)

infighting
infyting

infiltrate
dringe in, infiltrerre

infiltration
indringing, infiltraasen

infinite
unendig

infinitive
(gram) infinitiv

infinity
unendigness

infirm
wiek, swac, sheikig, unsteddig

infirmary
sickhousling, sicruem, sictimmer

infirmity
gebrec, wiekness

inflame
feroersacke, sturre up, sette aan fyer (brand),
bekindele, meike greiter (stranger)

inflammation
infleiming, swelling

inflammatory
upsturrish, upryend

inflate (air)
pumpe up, bloewe up; (prices)
dryve up

inflation
inflaasen, upswelling

inflationary
inflaasenish, updryvend

inflect
turne, bende; (gram) inflecterre

inflexibility
unbendbaarness, unflecsbaarness

inflection
turning, bending; **(gram)** inflecsen

inflexible
unbendbaar (-sum)

inflict
leye aan, bringe tue, beleide aan

influence
(n) swey (v) havve swey, hoelde

influential
sweyritch, sweyhoeldend

influx
infloew

inform
betyde, beryte, bringe (givve) tydings

inform against
sprecke agenst (teigen), denunserre

informal
unweyset

informality
informaliteit

informant
(reporter) beryter; aanclaager, teigensprecker (wid-)

information
kennisgivving, beryting, tydings, informaasen

informative
lerrnsum, informativ

informed
belytend

informer
teigensprecker (wid-), aanclaager

infrastructure
undergurd, underley, underpinning

infrequent
seldum, unoft(en)

infringe
breike in aan, breike yn laaw (wet)

infuriate
meike angrig (torn, wueden)

ingenious
findingritch, ingeinish, fernuftig

ingenuity
findingritchness, ingeinishness

ingest
teike (nyme) in

ingraft
(n) implant (v) implante

ingratitude
ungreitfulness, untankfulness

ingredient
bestanddiel, tuetaaten

ingrown
ingroewn

inhabit
bewoene

inhabitable
bewoenbaar

inhabitant
bewoener

inhalant
(adj) inbrietend (n) inbrieter, inaademer

inhalation
inbrieting, inaademing

inhale
briete in, inaademe

inhaler
inbrieter, inaademer

inharmonious
inharmoenish

inherit
errve

inheritance
errfness, oevererrving

inhibit
ferhindere, teigenhoelde (wid-), hoelde bac, underdrucke

inhibition
ferhindring, hemming

inhospitable
ungestlig, ungestfrie; (climate) berren, ferbidden

inhouse
inhous- (comb. form)

inhuman
unmenslig, unfrendlig, haartless

inhumane
inhumaan

inhumanity
unmensligness

initial
(adj) furst, begin-(comb. form), aanfanglig (n)
foerletter, aanfangsbuekstav, beginletter

initially
aanfangs, aanfanglig

initiate
inwyde, undernyme

initiation

inwyding

initiative
inissiativ

inject
inspritse, inspurte

injection
inspritsing, inspurting

injudicious
unwys, unferstandig

injure
haarme, wuende, ferletse

injurious
haarmful, ferletsig

injury
haarm, wuend, ferletsing

injustice
unrytigness, unferrness

inlay
inley

inmate
inmeit, bewoener

in memoriam
aantinken, errinnering

ink
ink

inkling
inkling, hint

inland
inland

in-laws
inlaaws, shienkin

inmost
inmoest

inn
inn, gesthous

innards
innerds

innate
inborn

inner
inner

inner city
innerstad

inner ear
innerier

innermost
innermoest

inning

(baseball)
inning

innkeeper
innkieper

innocence
ungilt, unshuld

innocent
ungiltig, unshuldig

innovate
fernuewe

innovation
fernuewing

innovator
fernuewer

innuendo
hint, tuespelling, innuendow

innumerable
untelbaar

inoculate
inente

inoculation
inenting

inocuous
unhaarmful, unshaadig, haarmless

inoffensive
unshaadelig, haarmless

inoperable
(med) inopererrbaar; unwurkbaar

inorganic
unorgaanish

inpatient
inhouspassent, inpassent

input
input

inquest
detundersieking, lykshouwing

inquire
frigge after

inquire into
undersieke, smie

inquiry
frig, undersieking

inquisition
(eccl)- Incwisissen; undersieking

inquisitive
nuewsgriedig, wityfrig

insane
mad, mindsic

insanity
madness, mindsicness

insatiable
unbefridbaar

inscription
inscript, inwryting

inseam
insiem

insect
insect, gnat

insecticide
insectkiller, insectfergift

insectivore
insectieter

insecure
unsecker

insecurity
unseckerness

inseminate
besiede

insensible
ungefielig, gefielless

insensitive
gefielless, unfielend

inseparable
unfersunderbaar, untrenbaar

insert
putte in, insieme, insette

insertion
input, insieme, inset

in-service
wurklinkt

inside
insyd

insider
insyder

insight
insyt

insignificant
unbedydend, mieningless

insincere
unupryt

insinuate
hinte, insinuerre

insinuation
hint, insinuaasen

insipid
dul, lyfless

insist
hoelde tue, aandringe

insistance
aandringen

insistent
dringend

insofar
insofaar

insole
insoel

insolence
unoerbydigness, unhofligness

insolent
unoerbydig, unhoflig

insoluable
unluesbaar

insolvable

See **insoluable**

insomnia
slieplessness

insomuch
insomutch

inspect

undersieke, besie,
beferre, inspecterre

inspection
undersieking, besieing, beferring, inspecsen

inspector
undersieker, besieyer, beferrder, inspector

inspiration
besoeling, inspiraasen

inspire
besoele, inspirerre

instep
instep

instigate
spurre aan, uphitse

instigation
uphitsing

instill
ferdraape, inbueseme, putte in (intue)

instillation
ferdraapness, inbuesemness

instinct
instinct

instinctive
instinctiv

institute
(n) instituet (v) instelle

institution
instelling, instituesen

institutional
instituetish

institutionalize
ferinstituetishe

instruct
underwyse, belerrne, tieche

instruction
underwys, belerrning

instructive
lerrnsum, instructiv

instructor
instructor, belerrner, tiecher

instrument
(mus) instrument

instrumental
instrumentaal

instability
unsteddigness, unbestendigness

instable
unsteddig, unbestendig

install
installe, instalerre

installation
instalaasen

installment
installing

instance
for instanz, foerbild, instanz

instant
(short period of time) - ygerblink, instant

instantaneous
unmiddelig

instantly
in yn ygerblink, instantlig

instead
insted

insubordinate
teigenweldish, widweldish

insubordination
teigenweldishness, widweldishness; (mil)
insubordinaasen

insuffiency
unfulduendness, ungenuegenness

insufficient
unfulduend, ungenuegend, ungenueg

insular
yland (comb. form)

insolate
isolerre

insulation
isolerring

insulator
isolaator

insulin
insulin

insult
(n) bismer, belydiging (v) belydige

insulting
bismerful, belydig, bismerlig

insurance
ferseckring

insure
ferseckere

insured
ferseckerd

insurer
ferseckerder

insurgence
uprysing

insurgent
(adj) uprysend (n) upryser, upstandeling

insurmountable
unoevercuemlig

insurrection
uprysing

insusceptible
unsweyd, unberuerbaar

intact
fulstandig, intaakt, gaaf

intake
inteik

intangible
unberuerbaar

interger
gehoel, getel

integral
gehoel, fulcuemen, integraal

integrate
blende, integrerre

integrity
sundness, uprytness, integriteit

intellect
ferstand, intelect

intellectual
(adj) ferstandlig, intelectu'el

intelligence
ferstand, intelligenz

intelligent
ferstandig, intelligent

intelligible
ferstandbaar

intend
foertinke, beduele, planne

intense
swyt, strang, haftig, intenz

intensify
ferstaarke, intensiferre

intensity
haftigness, intensiteit

intent
foertaat, foersetting, intent

intention
foernymen; goel

interaction
wisselwurking

intercede
cueme betwien, sprecke for (aan behaaf av)

interception
cut-av, offang

interceptor
ofcutter, offanger

intercession
tussencuemst

intercept
cutte av, halte, stoppe, offange

interchange
(n) wissling (v) wisele

interchangeable
wisselbaar

intercollegiate
tussenscuelig

intercom
oeverferbinder, intercom

intercontinental
tussencontinent (comb. form),
intercontinentaal

intercourse
imgang, ferkerr; (sex) sex (secs), copulaasen

interdict
(n) ferboed (v) ferbidde

interdiction
ferboed

interest
(n) belangstelling; (fin) intrest (v) stelle (teike)
yn, belang in

interesting
belangweikend, interessant

interfere
cueme betwien, mingele in, interferre

interference
tussencuemst, inmingling

interim
tussentyd

interior
(adj) inner (n) inland

interjection
tussencast, outruep

interloper
indringer

interlude
tussenspel, interlued

intermarriage
tussenwedloc

intermarry
tussenwedde

intermediate
tussen- (comb. form)

intermediary
(adj) tussengoewend (n) tussenpersoen

interminable
unendend, endless

intermission
tussentyd, underbreiking

intermittent
tussenbroeken

intern
(n) interrn, underdoctor

intersection
crossing

interstate
interstaat

intervene
cueme betwien

intervention
tussencuemst, bemiddling

interview
(n) befraaging, intervuew (v) befraage,
intervuewe

internal
inwendig, innerlig

internal medicine
internaal medisien

internal revenue
regerringincuem, taxincuem (tacs-)

international
internasionaal, tussenlanden

internationalize
internasionaliserre

internship
interrnship

interpose
tussenplaatse

interpret
fertolke, fercliere

interpretation
fertolking, fercliering

interpreter
fertolker

interracial
interrasiaal, interrassig

interrogate
ferhiere, underfraage

interrogation
ferhier, underfraaging

interrogator
ferhierder, underfraager

interrogatory
ferhier, fraagend

interrupt
breike in (aan), cutte av, underbreike

interruption
underbreiking

interscholastic
tussenscuelig

intersect
crosse

intestate
sonder testament, testamentless

intestines
ingewanden (v) interrne

intimacy
fertrouwness; (sexual) intimiteit

intimate-1
fertrouwlig; (sexual) intiem

intimate-2
hinte

intimidate
becouwe, befiere, intimiderre

intimidation
becouwing, befiering, intimidaasen

into
intue

intolerable
unberrbaar, unstandbaar

intolerance
unferberrsum-, ness, unferstandsumness, intoleranz

intolerant
unferberrsum, unferstandsum, intoleraant

intonation
toenfal

intoxicant
bedrunkend

intoxicate
bedrunke

intoxicating
bedrunkig

intoxication
bedrunken ness

intra-
(prefix) inner-, binnen-

intractable
unhandelbaar

intransigent
intransigent

intransitive
(gram) intransitiv

intrastate
innerstaat (binnen-)

intravenous
inneraadrig, (binnen-)

intrepid
unfershrocken, boeld, fierless

intricate
ingewickeld, compliserrt

intrigue
(n) intrieg (v) fasinerre

intrinsic
intrinsic

intro-
(prefix) inner-, binnen-

introduce
foerstelle+, inleye, introduserre, liede in;
(persons) presenterre
+ Forstelle can be used to introduce onesself.

introduction
inlieding, foerstelling, presenterring

introductory
inliedend

introvert
inturner, introverterrter

introverted
inturnd, introverterrt

intrude
indringe self, breike in aan

intruder
indringer

intrusion
indringing

intrusive
indringerig

intuition
intuissen

invigorate
ferstaarke, cwickene, fercwicke

inundate
oeverfloewe mid, oeverstrieme mid

inundation
overfloewing, oeverstrieming

invade
binnenfalle, duewe yn infal

invalid-1
(adj) ungeldig

invalid-2
(n) cranker

invalidate
meike ungeldig

invalidity
ungeldigness

invaluable
unshatbaar

invariable
unferanderlig

invasion
infal, invaasen

invent
outfinde, tinke up, ferzinne

invention
outfinding, ferzinsel

inventor
outfinder

inventory
(n) stoctelling, bestandlist (v) teike stoctelling (bestandlist)

inversion
imsetting, inverrsen

invert
imsette, imstelle, imkerre

invertebrate
(adj) bacboenless (n) unbacboner,
ungewerrfeld

invest
investerre, belegge

investigate
undersieke

investigation
undersieking

investigator
undersieker, detectiv, truetfinderinvestment,
belegging

investor
belegger

invigorating
fercwickend

invincible
unoeverwinlig, unoevercuembaar

invisible
unsytbaar

invitation
inlading, outniedeging

invite
ladde in, outniedige

invocation
aancalling (-rueping)

invoice
factuer

invoke
calle aan, aanruepe

involuntary
unwillend, unfriewillig

involve
infoelde, ferwickele

invulnerable
unhaarmbaar, unwuendbaar

inward
inwey, innerlig, inwendig

iodine
yodien

ion
ion

Iowa
Iowa

Iran
Iraan

Iranian
(adj/n) Iraanish (n) Iraaner

Iraq
Iraak

Iraqi
(adj/n) Iraakish (n) Iraaker

irate
tornig

Ireland
Ierland

Irene
Irien

irrefutable
unwerrlegbaar

irregular
unreigelmaatig

irrelevant
nit tuepaslig

irreperable
unherrstelbaar

irresistible
unwerrstaanbar

irresponsible
unanserlig

irresponsibility
unanserligness

irretrievable
unherrstelbaar

irreverent
unerrbiedig, respectless

irrigate
bewaatere

irrigation
bewaatring

Iris
Yris, Iries

irksome
urksum, boddersum, errgerlig

Irma
Ierma

iron
(n) ysen (v) ysene

ironic(al)
iroenish

irony
iroenie

irrational
unreidelig, irasionaal

irreconcilable
unferynigbaar, unfersoenlig

irredeemable
unbaccuepbaar, unherrstelbaar

irreducible
unlessenbaar, unfeloewerbaar

irritable
prickelbaar

irritate
prickele

irritating
pricklend

irrupt
burste

irruption
burst(ing)

Irwin
Errwin

is
due bie

Isaac
Isaak, Ysaak

Isabel(la)
Isabel(la)

-ish
(suffix) -ish

Islam
Islaam

Islamic
Islaamish

island
yland

-ism
(suffix) -isem

isobar
isobaar

isolate
ofsundere, isolerre

isolation
ofsundring, isolerring

Israel
Israel

issue
(n) outgang, outlet, outcuem, number, cwestaasen (v) goewe, passe, floewe out, cueme out, putte fort, ende in

-ist
(suffix) -ist -er, -or, -end

isthmus
landengt

it
it (nominative) dit (accusative)

Italian
(adj) Itallish (n) Italler, (language) Itallish

italicize
cursiverre

italics
cursivwrit

Italy
Itallie

itch
(n) itch (v) itche

item
aartikel, melding

itemize
liste

iterate
seye agen (anuew), nuwseye, herrhaalen

itinerant
weyferrder

itinerary
weyferrplan, reisbewryting

its
its, senners

itself
itself, self

Ivan
Ivaan, Yvan

ivory
ivoer

ivy
yvie

-ize
(suffix) -iserre

j-q

juror
bewys'hierder

kidnap
weyliede

kingdom
ryk

know (n)
ken

know-how
ken

knowingly
wittinglig

krypton
cripton

laced (v)
stringe up

lady-like
leidielig

language
tasal

lather
laader

law-abiding (wet-)

lawyer
(wet-)

lawbreaker
lawbreiker (wet-)

Leslie
Lesli (m), Leslier (f)

Liberia
Liberrie

linger
linggere

lingo
linggow

linguist
taalcundiger (-crafter)
related:
undertaal
blended taal
taalcundig
taalwittenship

linotype
linnotiep

listless
listless

literacy
(leis-)

literal
literasal

livelihood
(n) aanspreeckin

locution
sprecwey

loiter
linggere

161

loquacious
sprecsum

loudspeaker
loudsprecker

lucrative
winstgivvend

lunar month
muenmoenat

Lynn
Linn (m/f)

made-up
maakt-up

ma'am
guedfrouw

mackeral
maccrel

made
maakt

mail box
postbox (-cs)
mailcarrier
postberrder

man-made
manmaaakt

mandatory
behestgivvend

may
mey

meal-1 (food)

mercenary
geldunderfangen

merciful
baarmhaartig

merciless
unbaarmhaartig

mercuril
merrcuri'el

megaherrtz

metal
metaal

metalic
metaalish

metaphor
sprec

milk sugar
milksueger

mineral
mineraal

misery
wons'helt

mispronounce
misoutsprecke

misssionary
bekerrlingpriester

modal (ling)
modaal

mode
moed
moenats'halt

monologue
alynsprec

Moslem
Islaamish

mountaineer
berrgbewoener, berrgclymer
muederlig

Muslem
Islaamer

mute
unsprecbaar

mutineer
mueteder

mutinous
mueterish

mutiny
(n) muetery, (v) muetere

my
myn

mythological
mitoloegish

national
nasionaal

Nel
Nell

nestling
nestling

next-door
nextdoer (necst-)

Nightingale
nightengale

nominal
nominaal

normal
normaal

Norse
N ors

notion
noessen

noverna
nyndeygebeds

nullify
ungeldige

numerous
telritch

obstruct
hindere

oppose
sprecke agenst

or
oer

organist
organpleyer

ought
aat

ourselves
aarselven, ouwerselven

overlook
oeverlueke

overpass
oeverwey

pain
(n) eik, (v) eike

painful
eikig

paint
(n) peint, (v) peinte

painter
peinter, peinting

palatial
palataal

parliament
paarlament

particular
spesiaal

Paul
Poll

peasant
bouwer

penicillin
penisillin

persecute
ferfaalowe

pharmacy
faarmasie

phenomenal
fenomenaal

philanthropic
filantroepish

pioet
afestness

plaza
winkelgruep

plenty
(adj) genuegen, (n) genuegen

plural
(n) pluraal

pollinator
dustspredder

preserve
(n) dierkiepsted

presumption
fermueding

preview
furstfertoening

prior
errlig

probation
probaasen

phraseology
(sprec-) winstgivvend

prosecutor
ferfaalower

proceeds
inteik

prodical
ferswendrish

profitable
winstbringend

pronounce
sprecke out

pronouncement
outsprecking

pronouncement
outsprec

prophylactic
shied

Proserpina (myth)
Proserrpina

prosthesis
cunstlig lim

precarious
unsecker

precious
costbaar

Psalter
Salmbuek

premiere
(theather) furstshoewing

pulsation
pulserring

pure
clien, ryn (-est)

purify
rynige

puritan
ryniger

purity
rynigness

in pursuit of
aan hunt for, on hubt for

quarrell
(v) breike
quell

Quadrangl
fuerhuek

S

Sabbath
Saabat, restdey

Saber
saabel

sabotage
(n) sabotaag (v) saboterre

saboteur
sabotoer

saccharin
saccarin

sacerdotal
priesterlig

sack-1
(n) sac, fettels

sack-2
(v) plundere

sacrament
sacrament

sacramental
(adj) sacramentish (n) sacramenting

sacred
hoelig

sacrifice
(n) offer, ofring, geblot (v) offere (up), gebiede

sacrificial
gebiedish

sacrilege
sacrileg, hoeligskennis

sacrilegious
hoeligskennend

sacristy
sacristie

sad
sad, druef

sadden
saddene, bedrueve

saddle
saddel

sadness
sadness, druefness

safari
safaarie

safe
(adj) fylig, betrouwbaar, secker (n) fylignessbox(–cs)

safe and sound
gesund en wel

safety
fyligness, seckerness

safety belt
reddingsbelt

saga
saaga

sail
(n) seil (v) seile

sailboat
seilboet

sailor
seilor, matroes

saint
(adj) hoelig (n) hoelig

sake
(motive, benefit) seik

salad
salaat

salamander
saalamander

salary
saalarie, gehalt

sale
seil

sale
seil, fercuep

salesmanship
seilsmanship, fercuepership

salesperson
fercueper

saline
(adj) salthoeldend

saliva
spit

salivary
spit (comb. Form), spittig

salivate
spitte

sallow
sallow

salmon
laaks

salon
salon, greithal

saloon
baar, bierhal (-hous)

salt
salt

salty
saltig

salute
(n) handgrieting (v) handgriete

salvage
(n) berrging (v) berrge

salvation
redding (rel) heil, zaaligmeiking

salve
salf, balsem

same
seim

sample
(n) proeb, munster (v) proebe, bemunstere

Samuel
Sammuel

sanctified
ferhoeligd

sanctify
ferhoelige

sanctimonious
shynferhoelig

sanction
(n) sanksen, becractiging (v) sanksenerre, becractige

sanctity
hoeligness

sanctuary
hoeligdum, shelterhous

sand
(n) sand (v) sande

sandal
sandel

sandpaper
sandpapier

sandwich
sandwitch

sandy
sandig

sane
mindheltig

sang
(pt. of sing) did sing

sanitary
higienish, saniterr

sanitation
higien, sanitaasen

sanity
mindheltigness, saniteit

sank
(pt. of sink) did sinke

Sanskrit
Sanscriet

Sap
sap

Sapphire
safier

Sarah
Saara

Sarcasm
sarcaasem

Sarcastic
sarcaastish

Sardine
sardien

Satan
Saatan, Devvil

Satanic
sataanish

Satellite
saateliet

satirical
satierish

satirist
satierist

satirize
satariserre, heckele

satisfaction
befriddiging, tuefriddenness

satisfactory
befriddigend

satisfy
befriddige, tuefridde

Saturday
Saaturdey

saturate
soeke

saturation
soeking

sauce
saas

saucer
undercup

Saudi Arabia
Saadi Arabien

Sauerkraut
souwercrout

sauna
saana, souna

sausage
wurst

savage
(adj) wild, brutal, (n) wilder, brutaaler

save
(n - sports) seiv, (v) (rescue) redde, nerre, (general) beware, borge, (money) (be)spare, (sports) seive, ferhindere

saving
(adj) bewaarend

savings account
spaarrecning

savior
(rel) Heiland, Zaaligmeiker

saw
(tool) saaw

saw
(past tns of **see**) did sie

sawdust
saawdust

sawhorse
saawhors

Saxon
(adj) Sacsish, Saxish, (n) Sacser, Saxer, (language) Sacsen, Saxen

Saxophone
sacsofoen, saxofoen

say
seye

saying
seyen, seying

scab
(n) scab, (v) scabbe (oever)

scaffolding
geruest, styger

scald
brande

scale-1
(music) tonlyter, (ratio) metstaf, (for weighing) weitteller

scale-2
(of fish) shuep

scalp
(n) scalp, (v) scalpe

scandal
scandal

scandalize
scandaliserre

scandalous
scandalig

scatter
scattere, struewe, spredde

scene
(theater) tonel, sien

scenery
tonel, landskeip, bacdrop

scenic
tonel- (comb. form), landskeipig, shien

scent
(n) smel, guer, (v) smelle, rykene

sceptic
(adj) septish

schedule
(n) taabel, plan, tydplan, (v) planne, faststelle

schematic
skemaatish

scheme
(n) skeima, plan, (v) beraame

schemer
skeimer, intrigaant

schism
skisma

schizophrenic
(adj) skitsofren (n) skitsofrennic

scholar
upwitter, gelerrter, bueker, witshipper

scholarly
gelerrt, witshiplig

scholarship (ability)
gelerrtness, (fin aid) stipendie, gelerrtnessgeld, witshipligness

scholastic
scolastish

school-1
(educ) scuel

school-2
(crowd) scoel

school board
scuelbord

schoolhouse
scuelhous(-bilding)

schooling
scueling, educaasen

schoolteacher
scueltiecher, underwyser

schwa
shwaaw

sciatic
iskiaas

sciatica
iskiaasa

science
wittenship

scientific
wittenshiplig

scientist
wittenshipper

scissors
shaar

sclerosis
tissuehardning, scleroes

scold
scoelde

scolding
scoelding

scoop
(n) scuep, (v) scuepe

scope
(range, area) imfang, (comb. form) -scoep

score
(n) telling, scoer, (v) scoere

scorpion
scorpioen

Scot
Scot

Scotland
Scotland

Scottish
Scottish

Scotsman
(m/f) Scotter

Scott
(male name) Scott

scour
scouwere

scout
ferkenner

boyscout
patfinder

scrap
(n) scrap, (v) scrappe

scrape
(n) screip, (v) screipe

scratch
(n) scratch, (v) scratche

scream
(n) scriem, (v) scrieme

screen
(n) screen, (v) scriene (av, in)

screw
(n) scruew, (v) scruewe

scribble
(n) scribble, (v) scribbele

script
handwryting, script

scrotum
testikelbag, hoedensac

scrub
(n) scrub, (v) scrubbe

scruple
gewettensbeswaar,

scrupulous
gewissenhaft, angstfallig

sculptor
beldbouwer

sculpture
beldbouwcunst

sea
sie

seacoast
siecoest

seafarer
sieferrder, sieman

siefaring
sieferrend

sea gull
siefoul, siefoegel, siegul

sea horse
siehors

seal-1
(zool) siel, siehund

seal-2
(mark) (n) siegel, (v) besiegele

sealant
fersiegler

seam
(n) siem, (v) sieme

seaman
sieman, matroes, seilor

seamanship
siemanship

séance
seanz, spiritistish sitting

search
(n) sieking, dursieking, (v) sieke

search for
sieke after

search party
siekgruep

season
yier(ge)tyd, seisoen

seasonable
gepast, geshict, tydlig

seasoning
cryden

seat
(n) siet, sietplaats, (v) teike (have) yn siet, sitte (doun)

seat belt
sietbelt

seating
sieting

seaway
siewey

seaworthy
siewurdig

secede
tredde out, widdraawe av

secession
widdraaw, widdraawing

seclude
hyde, isolerre, shutte av

secluded
hidden

seclusion
isolerring, ofshutting

second
(number) twied, ander, (time) ygerblink

secondary
(school) hyscuel; (gen'l) seconderr

Second Coming
(rel) Cristbac-cuemen, Twiedbaccuemen

secondhand
twiedhand, unnuew, foer(ge)brykt

secondly
in die twied plaats

secrecy
gehymhoelding

secret
gehym

keep a secret
kiepe (hoelde), yn gehym

secret police
gehympolies

secret sevice
gehymundersiek

secretary
secreterr

secretion
gehymkieping, (-hoelding)

secretive
bac'hoeldend, gehymkiepend, gehymhoeldend

sect
sect

section
ofdeiling, secsen

sector
sector

secular
weldig, weldlyk

secularism
weldigness, weldlykness

secularize
ferweldige, seculariserre

secure
(adj) secker, bemytig, (v) fastmeike, seifmeike

security
seckerness, bemytigness

sedan
fuerdoeraatow

sedative
(adj) beruewigend, calmerend, (n) beruewigendmiddel, calmermiddel

sedition
upstand

seduce
ferlyde, spanne

seduction
ferlyding

seductive
ferlydelig

see-1
(power of vision) sie

see about
sie about

see after
sie after

see off
sie av

see through
sie duer

see to
sie tue

see-2
(rel) bisperdum

seed
(n) sied, (v) siede

seeing
sieing, syt

seek
sieke

seem
sieme, shyne

seemingly
shynbaar

seep
siepe

seepage
siepen

seer
foreteller

see-through
shier, duersytig

seesaw
siesaaw

seethe
siede

segment
segment

segregate
(vt) ofsondere, trenne, (vi) ofsondere self

segregation
ofsondring, trenning

seismic
seismish

seismograph
seismograaf

seize
graspe, grype, fernyme, faane, confiskerre, befange

seizure
(med) beruert; (gen'l) gryping, fernyming

seldom
selden

select
chuese, picke (out), kiese out, ferkiese

selection
chuesing, ferkiesing

selenium
selennium

self
self

self-
(pfx) self-

self-acting
selfwurkend

self-assurance
selffertrouwen

self-centered
selfish

self-confident
selffertrouwen

self-conscious
selfbewust

self-control
selfbeherrsing

self-defense
selffertydiging

self-discipline
selfdissiplien

self-educated
selfbeshaaft

self-employed
selfhyered, selfstandig

self-esteem
selflof, selfbehef

self-evident
oepensytlig

self-help
selfhelp

self-government
selfregerring

self-hypnosis
selfhipnoes

self-image
selfwurt

selfish
selfish

selfishness
selfishness

selfless
selfless

self-made
selfmaakt

self-pity
selfmidlyden

self-respect
selferrbied, gevuel

selfrighteous
selfgeryt

self-rule
selfregerring

self-taught
selftaat

sell
selle, fercuepe

seller
seller, fercueper

Selma
(fem name) Selma

sellout
(n) selout

sell out
(v) selle out

selves
selvs

semantics
wurdstuedie

semen
siedkiem

semester
semester

semi-
(pfx) half-, haaf-

semiannual
halfyierig, (haaf-)

semicircle
halfsierkel, (haaf-)

semicolon
halfcoloen (haaf-)

semiconscious
halfawerr (haaf-)

seminar
seminaar

seminary
goestligeruniversiteit, seminaarie

Semite
Semiet

Semitic
Semietish

Semitism
Semitissem

semitropical
semitroepish

Senate (US)
Upperhous, Upperlaawmeikerhous, (Roman council) Senaat

send
sende

send away
sende awey

send down
sende doun

send for
sende for, gelange

send in
sende in

send up
sende up

Senegal
Senegaal

senile
senile

senior
(adj) hyranken, (n) oeldster, twelvstepper

seniority
hyer rank, tydlengterness

sensation
(feeling) gefiel, sensassen

sense
(meaning) betokening, sens; (feeling) gefiel

common sense
ferstand

in a sense
in yn wey (miening)

make sense
havve miening, bie ferstandbaar

senseless
gefielless, ungefielig; goelless, ungoelig

sensible
ferstandig, maarkbaar

sensitive
gefielig, fyngefielig

sensitivity
fyngefieligness

sensor
gefieler

sensual
zinlig, gefielig

sent
(ling) did sende (pt); sent (pt part)

sentence
(gram) setning; (n) (judgment) fonnis, oerdiel
(v) fonnisse

sentiment
gefiel, fieling

sentimental
sentimentel

sentimentality
sentimenteliteit

sentinel
waacher

sentry
waacher

separable
trenbaar, shydbaar

separate
(adj) getrent, geshyden (n) trenne, shyde,
tuenyme

separation
trenning, shyding, gedoel

separator
ofshyder, roemofshyder

September
September

septic
septish

septic tank
swiltank, septish tank

sequel
ferfolger

sequence
ferfolgerorder

Serbia
Serrbie

Serbian
(adj) Serrbish (n) (person) Serrber (language)
Serrbish

serenade
(n) serrenaad (v) bringe yn serrenaad

serene
unbewoegen, calm, gelasssen

serenity
unbewoegenness, gerlassenness

serf
wyel, tieow, trel

serfdom
wyelness, tieowness

sergeant
serrgent

serial
(adj) aangoewend (n) aangoewer, aanganger

serialize
meike intue yn aanganger

series
reiks, selffolger, serrie

serious
errnstig, errnst

seriousness
errnstigness

sermon
(RC) homelie (Prot) Bybelraad, pulpitsprec,
preik

serpent
sneik, slang

serrated
gezaagd

serum
serum

servant
bediender, wyel, tieower

serve

bediene, tieowe

service
bediening, tieowdum, teinship, dienst

servitude
slaaverny

serviceman
militerrder, reparerrder

service station
aatowstelling

serviette
napkin, serrvyet

serving
sherr, aandiel

servitude
slaaverny, strafwurk

session
sitting

set
(n) set (vt) sette, putte (vi) sette, haardene

Setback
(n) setback

set back
(v) sette bac

set down
(v) sette doun

set off
(v) sette av

set-up
(n) set-up

set up
(v) sette up

Setting
setting, imgivving, imweld

settle
settele

settlement
settling

settler
settler

seven
sevven

seventeen
sevventien

seventeenth
sevventient

seventh
sevvent

seventieth
sevventiget

seventy
sevventig

sever
ofsnyde, breike av

several
(adj/n) mennig, bissen

sew
soewe

sewer
soewer, waaterpyp

sewing
soewing

sex
(gender) geslact (copulation) sex (secs)

sexual
(adj) sexu'el (secsu'el) (comb.form) geslacts…

sexuality
sexualiteit (secs-)

shade
(n) sheid (v) sheide

shadow
(n) shaadow (V) shaadowe

shady
sheidig

shaft
shaft

shah
shaaw

shake
(n) sheik (v) sheike

shaker
sheiker

shaky
sheikig

shall
(obsolete form of **will**)

shallow
shallow, undiep

shaman
shaaman

shame
(n) sheim (v) sheime

shameful
sheimful

shameless
sheimless

shampoo
(n) shampuew (v) shampuewe

shamrock
Ierish cloever, shamroc

shank
(anat) shank

Shannon
(fem name) Shannen

shape
(n) sheip, form (v) sheipe, forme

shapeless
sheipless, formless

shapely
sheiplig

shard
shaard

share
(n) sherr, aandiel (vt) sherre, ferdiele (vi) sherre, diele

shareholder
sherrhoelder, aandielhoelder

shark
(zool shark, hy

Sharon
(fem name) Sherren

sharp
(adj) sharp, taart

sharpen
shaarpene, fershaarpe

shatter
shattere, fersplinte

shatters
shatters

shatterproof
shatterpruef

shave
(n) sheiv (v) sheive

shaver
sheiver

shaving cream
sheivcriem

she
shie

she-
(prefix) shie-

shear
shiere

shears
shiers

sheath
shied

shed-1
(bldg.) shed

shed-2
(v) shedde

sheen
shien

sheep
(sing, pl) shiep

sheepish
shiepish

sheer-1
(adj) shier

sheer-2
(n) shier (v) shiere

sheet
shiet

sheeting

shieting

sheik (h)
sheik

shelf
shelf (plural: shelven, shelfs)

shell
(n) shel (v) shelle

shellack
shelac

shelter
(n) shelter (v) sheltere, betetche, behyde

shelve
shelve

shelving
shelving

shepherd
shepherrder

sherbet
sherrbet

sheriff
sherrif, (col) sherrf

shield
(n) sheld (v) shelde

shift
(n) shift (v) shifte

shiftless
shiftless

shifty
shiftig

shimmer
(n) shimmer (v) shimmere

shine
(n) shyn (v) shyne

shingle
(n) (wood slat) shingel (v) shingele

shingles
gurdelblisters

shining
shyning

shiny
shynig

ship
(n) ship (v) shippe

-ship
(suffix) -ship

shipment
fershipping, laading

shire
shyer

shirk
shurke

Shirley
(fem name) Shurlie

Shiver
(n) shivver (v) shivvere

shock-1
(n) (emotion) shoc (v) shocke

shock-2
(grain) shoc

shock absorber
shocferbreiker

shocking
shockig

shoe
(n) shuew (v) shuewe

shoehorn
shuewhorn

shoelace
shuewstring

shoestring
shuewstring

shone
(past pt of **shine**) shoen

shook
did sheike

shoot
shuete

shop
(n) shop (v) shoppe

shopkeeper
shopkieper, shopoewner

shoplift
shoplifte

shoptalk
shopsprec (-taak)

shore-1
(water's edge) shoer

shore up
shoere up

shore leave
shoerliev

short
(adj) short (n) short (v) shorte

shortage
shortfall, shorting

short circuit
shortluep

short-circuit
shortluepe

shortcoming
shortcueming

shorten
shortene

shortening
shortning

shorts
shorts

shorthand
shorthand

short-handed
shorthanded

short-lived
shortlivd

shortly
shortlig

short-sighted
shortsyted

short-tempered
cwicangrig, (-tornig)

short- term
shorttyd

short-winded
shortwinded

shot
(n) shot, shueter

shot
(pt of **shoot**) did shuete (past pt. of **shoot**)
shot

should
(pt modal aux of **shall**) shud

shoulder
(n) shoelder (v) shoeldere

shouldn't
shudnie (contraction for shud nit)

shout
(n) shout, ruep (v) shoute, ruepe

shove
(n) shuev, push (v) shueve, pushe

shoevel
(n) shuevel (v) shuevele

show
(n) shoew (v) shoewe

show-off
(n) shoew-of

show off
(v) shoewe av

show up
shoewe up, atwie, fershyne

shower
(n) shouwer (v) shouwere, teike yn shouwer

showing
shoewing

shown
(pt. part of **show**) shoewn

showroom
shoewruem, shoewtimmer

shred
(n) shred (v) shredde

shrewd
shrued

shriek
(n) shriek (v) shrieke

shrift
(confession and absolution by a priest), shrift

shrill
(n) shrill (v) shrille

shrimp
shrimp

shrine
shryn

shrink
(n) shrink (v) shrinke

shrinkage
shrinking

shrive
(hear confession and give absolution) shryve

shroud
shroud

Shrovetide
Shroevtyd (three days before Ash Wednesday)

shrubbery
shrubbrie

shrug
(n) shrug (v) shrugge

shuck
shucke

shudder
(n) shudder (v) shuddere

shuffle
(n) shuffel (v) shuffele

shun
shunne

shunt
(n) shunt (v) shunte

shut
(adj) shut (v) shutte, betyne

shutdown
shutdoun

shut down
shutte doun

shut-in
shut-in

shutoff
(n) shutof

shut off
(v) shutte av

shut up
shutte up

shuttle
(n) shuttel (v) shuttele

shy
(adj) shy, bashful, ferleigen

shy away
shye awey

shyness
shyness, bashfulness, ferleigenness

sibling
sibling

Siberia
Siberrie

Siberian
(adj) Siberrish (n) Siberrish

sibilant
(adj) sissend (n) sisclank

sic
(v) sicke

Sicilian
Sissiler

Sicily
Sissilie

sicken
sickene

sickle
sickel

sickly
siclig

sickness
sicness

sickroom
sicruem, sictimmer

side
(adj) syd (n) syd (v) syde

sideburns
sydburnen

side effect
(med) sydefect

sidestep
sydsteppe

sidestroke
(n) sydstroek (v) sydstroeke

siding
syding

sidewalk
sydwaak

sideways
sydweys

sideswipe
(n) sydswyp (v) sydswype

Sidney
(male name) Sidni

siege
(n) belegging (v) leye belegging tue

Siegfried
Siegfried

sift
sifte

sight
(adj) syt (n) syt (v) syte

sightless
sytless

sightseeing
sytsieing

sign
(n) toeken, bieken (v) undertoekene, wryte

signal
(n) sein, signaal (v) seine, signalerre

signatories
undertoekenaars, underwryters

signature
undertoekning, handtoeken

significance
miening, betoekenness, bedueling

significant
mieningful, fielbetoeknend

signify
miene, betoekene, beduele, bedyde

sign language
toekentaal

sign of the cross
toeken av die cros (rued)

sign of the Zodiac
toeken av die Zoediac

signpost
weyshoewer

silence
stilness, swy

silent
stil(lish), swygend; **be silent** gestille, bie stil;
remain silent swyge

silencer
gestiller

silhouette
(n) siluwet (v) siluwette

silk
silk

silken
silkene

silky
silkig

sill
sil

silly
sillig

silo
sielow, foddertouwer

silt
silt

silver
silver

silvery
silvrig

silverware
silverwerr

simian
aapactig, aapish

similar
alyk, lyk, oeveryncomstig

similarly
ingelyks, onlitch

similarity
lykness, oeveryncomst

simile
fergelyking

Simon
Siemon, Symen

simple
ynfoeldig, ynfaak

simplicity
ynfoeld, ynfaakness

simplify
ferynfoldige, ferynfaake

simplification
ferynfoeldiging, ferynfaaking

simply
ynfoeldig, ynfaak

simulate
foerwende, simulerre

simulation
foerwending, simulaasen

simulator
simulaator

simultaneous
gelyktydig, seimtydig

sin
(n) sin (v) sinne, gefierene

since
(prep, adv, conj) sinz

sincere
upryt, haartfelt

sincerity
uprytness

sinew
sinyuw

sinful
sinful

sinfulness
sinfulness

sing
singe

singe
fersenge, senge

singer
singer

single
(adj) unfertrouwd, unwed(ded) (n) ynkel (v)
ynkele

singular
ynkelfoeldig

sinister
ungunstig

sink
(n) sink (v) sinke

sinker
sinker

sinkhole
sinkhoel

sinner
sinner

sinus
holt, sinus

sinusitis
sinusswelling

Sioux
(North American Indian tribe) Suew

siphon
(n) heivel, sifon (v) heivele, draawe av, sifonne

Sir (sir)
myn herr

sire
(n) faader (v) faadere

siren
sienimf, foerwaarninghorn

sirloin
loincut, bestcut

sirup
See syrup

sister
sister, nun (rel)

sisterhood
sisterhued

sister-in-law
laawsister, shiensister

sit
sitte

sit back
sitte bac

sit-down
(adj/n) sitdoun

sit down
(v) sitte doun

sit-in
(n) sit-in

sit in
(v) sitte in

sit-up
(n) sit-up

sit up
(v) sitte up

site
ligging

sitter
sitter

sitting
sitting

situated
geset

situation
tuestand, situaasen

six
six, sics

sixteen
sixtien, sicstien

sixteenth
sixtient, sicstient (or noun + sixtien (sics-)

sixth
sixt, sicst (or noun + six (sics)

sixty
sixtig, sicstig

size
(n) greitness, number (imfang. format) (v) fergreite, mette

size up
ferdieme

skate
(n) skeit (v) skeite

skeleton
geraant, skelet

skeleton key
loeper, dietric, oepenal

skeptic
twyvler

sketch
(n) sketch (v) sketche

ski
(n) skie (v) skie, skieloepe

skid
(n) skid (v) skidde, slippe

skiing
skieloepen

skill
skil, geshic, becwaamness

skillful
skilful, geshict, becwaam

skilled
skild, geshict

skillet
frypan

skim
skimme

skim milk
skimmilk

skin
(n) skin, hyd (v) skinne

skinny
skinnig

skip
(n) skip (v) skippe

skipper (leader)
skipper

skirt
skurt ,roc

skittish
skittish

skoal
scoel, proesit

skull
skul, sheidel

skunk
skunk, stinkdier

sky
sky, himmel

sky blue
skybluew

skylark
skylaark

slack
(adj) slac (n) slac (v) slacke

slacken
slackene

slam
(n) slam (v) slamme

slander
(n) laster (v) belastere

slang
slang

slant
(adj) slant (n) slant (v) slante

slate
lystoen

slaughter
(n) slaater (v) slaatere

slaughterhouse
slaaterhous

Slav
(adj) Slaavish (n) Slaav

slave
(n) slaav, wyvel (v) slaave

Slavic
Slaavish

slay
sleye

sled
(n) sled (v) sledde, sledryde

sledding
sledding, sledryding

sledgehammer
sledghammer

sleep
(n) sliep (v) sliepe

sleeper
slieper

sleeping bag
sliepingbag

sleepless
sliepless

sleepwalker
sliepwaanderlaar

sleepover
(n) sliepoever

sleep over
(v) sliepe oever

sleepy
sliepig

sleet
(n) sliet (v) sliete

sleeve
sliev

sleigh
sley

slender
slender

sleuth
(n) detectiv, sluet, spurder (v) detecte, upspurde, unravvele

slew
sluew

slice
(n) slys (v) slyse

slick
slic

slicker
slicker, reinmantel

slide
(n) slyd (v) slyde

slide rule
slydlineaar

slight
(adj) slyt (n) slyt (v) slyte

slim
(adj) slim (v) slimme

slime
slym

slimy
slymig

sling
(n) sling (v) slinge

slink
slinke

slinky
slinkig

slip
(n) slip (all meanings) (v) slippe

slip-on
(n) slip-aan

slip on
(v) slippe aan

slipper
slipper

slippery
slipperig

slit
(n) slit (v) slitte

sliver
slivver

slogan
sloegan

slope
sloep

sloppy
sloppig

slot
sluf

slot machine
pleyatomaat, gambelatomaat

Slovak
(adj) Sloevaak (n-person) Sloevaak (n-language) Sloevaak

Slovakia
Slovaakie

Slovenia
Slovienie

Slovenian
(adj) Slovienish (n-language) Slovienish (n-person) Sloviener

slow
(adj./adv.) sloew, langsaam (v) sloewe (up, doun)

sly
sly

smack-1
(n-taste) smac (v- have a smack of) smacke

smack-2
(n-hit) smac (v-hit) smacke

small
smal, clyn, littel

small arms
smalweppens

small intestines
smalgut, smaldaarm

smallness
smalness

small talk
smalsprec

smallpox
smalpox, smalpocs

smart
(adj) smaart, intelligent; (rude) roew, unbeshaaft, unhoflig (v) (to feel pain) smaarte

smart alec
(k) smaartallec

smart off
smaarte av

smash
(n) smash (v) smashe

smattering
smattring

smear
(n) smier (v) smiere

smell
(n) (good, bad, neutral) smel (v) smelle

smelly
(bad) smellig

smidgen
smidgen

smile
(n) smyl (v) smyle

smirk
(n) smurk (v) smurke

smith
smit

smitten
smitten

smitten with
smitten mid

smock
smoc

smog
smog

smoke
(n) smoek, roek (vi, vt) smoeke (vi) roeke (vt) beroeke

smoker
smoeker, roeker

smoky
smoekig, roekig

smolder
(n) smoelder (v) smoeldere

smooth
(adj) smued (v) smuede

smooth over
smuede oever

smother
(vi, vt) smuedere

smudge
smudg

smug
smug

smuggle
smuggele

smuggler
smuggler

smut
smut

smutty
smuttig

snack
(n) snac (v) snacke

snag
(n) snag (v) snagge

snail
sneil

snake
(n) sneik, slang (v) sneike

snap
(n) snap (v) snappe

snare
(n) snerr, grien (v) snerre, griene

snarl-1
(n-growl) snaarl (v-growl) snaarle

snarl-2 (entanglement)
(n) snaarl (v) snaarle

snatch
(n) snatch (v) snatche

sneak
(adj) sniek (n) sniek (v) snieke

sneaker
snieker

sneaky
sniekig

snear
(n) snier (v) sniere

sneeze
(n) snies (v) sniese

snide
snyd

sniff
(n) snif (v) sniffe

snip
(n) snip (v) snippe

sniper
snyper

snippy
snippig

snoop
(n) snuep (v) snuepe

snore
(n) snoer (v) snoere

snorkel
(n) snorkel (v) snorkele

snow
(n) snoew (v) snoewe

snowball
(n) snoewbal (v) snoewballe

snowfall
snoewfal

snowflake
snoewfleik

snowdrift
snoewdrift

snowplow
snoewplouw

snowslide
snoewslyd

snowshoe
snoewshuew

snowstorm
snoewstorm

snowsuit
snoewcladding

snowy
snoewig

so
(all meanings) soew

so much the better
soew mutch die better

so to speak
soew tue sprecke (seye)

soak
(n) soek (v) soeke

soap
(n) soep (v) soepe

soapy
soepig

soar

hyglyde

sob
(n) sob (v) sobbe

sober
soeber, nucter

sobriety
soeberness, nucterness

sobriquet
nicneim, teikenneim

so-called
soew-cald

soccer
socker

socialbility
gezelligness

sociable
gezellig, fertreilig, sosiaal

social
(adj) gezellig

socialism
sosialissem

socialist
sosialist

socialize
sosialiserre

society
saamenlivving, feryniging; die hy (greit) weld

sociologist
sosioloeg(-ist)

sociology
sosialoegie

sock-1
(stocking) soc

sock-2
(hit) socke

socket
hollow

sod
sod

soda
soeda

sodium
soedie

sodomy
soedomie

sofa
soefa, sofaaw

soft
soft, wyk

softball
softbal

soft drink
softdrink

soft palate
softferhemmelt

software
softwerr

soil
grund, errt

sojourn
ferblyf

solace
(n) troest, ferlicting (v) fertroeste

solar
sun…(comb. form)

solarium
sunruem (-timmer)

solder
(n) soldersel (v) solder

soldier
soldaat

sole-1
alyn, ynig

sole-2
(foot) soel

solely
See sole-1

solemn
hoelig, plictig

solemnity
plictigness

solemnize
meike plictig; voltrecke (marriage)

solicit
fraage im, aske for, fersieke

solicitation
fersiek, aandringen

solicitor
notaaris; **Solicitor General** Solissitor Generaal

solid
nit hollow, tytpact steivig, solied

solidarity
solidariteit

solidify
stolle, consoliderrre, meike stolle

solidity
steivigness, soliditeit

solitary
alyn, ynig

solitude
ynsaamness

solo
(adj/n) soelow

so long
soewlang, tilsieagen, tilsieanuew, by

solstice
sunstilstand

solubility
upluesbaarness

soluble
upluesbaar

solution
fercliering, upluesing

solvability
luesbaarness, solvabiliteit

solvable
upluesbaar

solve
upluese, fercliere

solvency
solvabiliteit

solvent
(adj) solvent (n) upluesingsmiddei

Somali
(adj) Somaalish (n-person) Somaaler
(n-language) Somaalish

Somalia
Somaalie

some
suem

-some (suffix)
-sum

somebody
suemboedig, suemyn

someday
suemdey

somehow
suemhouw

somersault
byteling, oeverliep

something
suemting

sometime
(adj/adv) suemtyd

sometimes
suemtyms

someway
suemwey

somewhat
(adv) suemwat (n) suemwat

somewhere
suemwerr

son
soen

sonata
sonaata

song
sang

sonnet
sonnet

songster
sangster, singer

songwriter
sangwryter, compoeser

sonorous
clankful, clankritch, sonoer

soon
suen, snel, fruew

soot
suet

sooth
suet

soothe
suede

soothsayer
suetseyer, truetseyer

sophisticated
sofistikerrt

sophomore
twieder

soprano
sopraan

sorcerer
wisserd

sorcery
drycraft, witchcraft

sordid
durtig, smuttig, befould, laag

sore
(adj) soer, peinful (n) soer

sorority
sisterligness, sistership (-hued)

sorrow
saarow, sorg

sorrowful
saarowful, sorgful

sorry
saarig

Sorry!
Entshuldiging!

sort
(n) sort (v) sorte

sortie
cwicstryk; (single-plane mission) sortie

soul
soel

soulful
soelful

sound-1
(noise) gelyd, clank, swaying

sound-2
(healthy) sund

sound-3
(channel) sund

soundness
sundness; soliditeit

soundproof
gelydpruef

soup
suep

sour
souwer

source
wel, spring, upspring

south
(adj, adv,n) sout

South Africa
Sout Africa

South America
Sout Amerrica

South Carolina
Sout Caroliena

South Dakota
Sout Dacoeta

southeast
soutest

southeastern
soutestern

southeastward
soutestwey

southerly
souderlig

southerner
souderner

southward
soutwey

souvenir
kiepseik, suvenier, aandenken

sow-1
(zool) souw

sow-2
soewe

spa
hielbat, spaaw

space
ruemt, spaas, outerness

spaceraft
spaascraft(-ship), outerruemteship

spaceship
See spacecraft

spacious
geruemig

spade
(tool) speid; (card) piek

spaghetti
spagetti (It. pl.)

Spain
Spaan

Spaniard
Spaaner

Spanish
(adj) Spaanish (n- language) Spaanish

spare
(adj) sperr (n) sperr (v) sperre

sparke
(n) spaark (v) spaarke

sparkle
(n) spaarkel (v) spaarkele

sparrow
(zool) spaarow

sparse
tin, scatterd

spasm
cramp

spasmodic
crampactig

spatter
(n) spatter (v) spattere

spatula
spaatel

spawn
briede

spay
speye

speak

sprecke

speaker
sprecker

speaking
sprecken

spear
(n) spier (v) spiere

spearmint
peppermint

special
bisonder, sindrelig, spesiaal

specially
sindrelig

specialist
spesialist

speciality
spesialiteit

specie
spesies

specific
bestimt, genouw

specification
spesificaasen

specify
spesifiserre

specimen
foerbeld

spectacular
spectaculerr, grandioes

spectator
waacher, tueshouwer

specter
goest, spuek

spectral
goestlig

spectrum
spectrum

speculate
speculerre

speculation
speculaasen

speculator
speculant, speculaator

speech
spraak, taal

speechless
spraakless

speed
(n) spied, snelness, haast, cwicness

speedometer
spiedmetter, snelnessmetter

speed up
spiede up, fersnelle

speedy
spiedig, snel, haastig, cwic, fast

spell-1
(magic power) spel

spell-2
(lettering) buekstaffe, spelle

spell-3
(n-time) spel (v-work in place of another) spelle

spellbind
spelbinde, fasinerre

spelling
spelling, buekstaffing

spell out
fercliere

spend
spende, givve out

spendthrift
spendtrift

sperm
sperrm, sied

spermatozoon
sperrmaatazoid

spew
spuewe, braake

sphere
sferr

spherical
balformig, sferrish

spice
cryd, gewurts

spicy
gecryd, wurtsig

spider
spyder, webspinner

spin
(n) spin (v) spinne

spinach
spinaat

spinal
bacboen...(comb. form)

spine
bacboen, ruggeraat

spinster
spinster, unwed frouw

spiral
(adj) spiraalformig (n) spiraal

spire
spyer

spirit
goest

spiritual
goestlig

spiritualism
goestligness, spiritualiteit

spiritualist
goestligger, spiritualist

spiritualize
spiritualiserre

spit-1
(saliva-n) spit (expectorate-v) spitte

spit-2
(rod) spit

spite
wroc; **in spite of** trots

spiteful
gehessig, mien

splash
(n) splash (v) splashe

splatter
(n) splatter (v) splattere

spleen
milt

splendid
wuenderful, herrlig, practig splendorpract, lyster

splice
(n) split (v) splitte

splint
splint, cliev

splinter
(n) splinter (vi) splintere (vt) fersplintere

split
(n) splitsing (v) splitte

spoil
bederrvd, plundere

spoilage
beroeving, plundring

spoiled
bedorven

spoilsport
spielbederrver

spoke-1
(pt of speak) did sprecke

spoke
(of wheel) spoek

sponge
spons

spongy
sponsig

sponsor
(n) sponsor (v) stande in for, sponsere

spontaneous
spontaan

spoof
(n) spuef (v) spuefe

spook
(n) spuek, goest (v) spueke, staartele

spooky
spuekig, ierig, wierd

spool
spuel

spoon
(n) spuen (v) spuene

spoonful
spuenful

spoor
spoer

sporadic
sporaadish

sport
(adj) sport (n)sport, speiling

sporting
sports (comb. form) (e.g. sportswerr, sportswryter)

sportsmanship
sportsmanship

spot
(n) spot, flec, plaats (v) spotte, maarke (av)

spotty
geflect

spouse
eiger (m/f)

spout
(n) spout (v) spoute

sprain
(n) ferrecking (v) ferrecke

sprang
did springe

spray
(n) sprey (v) spreye

spread
(n) spred (v) spredde; did spredde

spring
(adj) spring (n) jump, liep; (origin) fruemer (well) waaterfruemer (season) spring, lengthen (v) springe, jumpe, liepe, bounde, ryse up, aryse

springtime
springtyd, lengten

springy
springig

sprinkle
(n) sprinkel (v) sprinkele

sprinkling
(n) sprinkling

sprint
(n) sprint (v) sprinte

sprite
elf

sprocket
sprocket

sprout
(n) sprout (v) sproute

spry
spry

spur
(n) spur (v) spurre

spurn
(n) spurn (v) spurne

spurt
(n) spurt (v) spurte

spy
(n) spioen (v) spionerre, spie aan

spying
spionaag

squad
gruep; (mil) underplatuen, scwaad

squadron
(mil) geshwaader

square
(adj) fuercant, rythuekig (n) fuercant (v) meike yn fuercant

square dance
fuercantdanz

squat
(adj) hielsitten, crouch (n) hielsit, crouch (v) hielsitte, crouche

squaw
scwaaw, Indiaanenfrouw

squeak
(n) scwiek (v) squieke

squeeze
(n) scwies (v) scwiese, drucke out

squid
scwid, tenaarmfish

squint
(n) shiel (v) shiele

squire
landherr

squirm
wriggele, wryde

squirrel
eikhorn

squirt
(n) sprits (v) spritse

stab
(n) stic (v) sticke

stability
stabiliteit

stabilization
stabilisaasen

stabilize
stabiliserre

stable
stabiel

stack
(n) stac (v) stacke

stadium
staadion, waacherssieting

staff
(stick) staf; (group of people) staf, gierd

stag
(adj) staag (adult male deer) staag

stage
(n) toneil, platform (v) fertoneile, performe

stagger
(n) stagger (v) staggere

stagnant
stilstaand

stagnate
stilstaane, stagnerre

stagnation
stilstand, stagnaasen

stain
(n) flec, spotting; sheim (v) beflecke; sheime

stainless
unbeflect

stair
(usu. pl.) sterrs, trep

staircase
sterrwey

stake
(n) steik (v) steike

stalactite
stalactiet, dripstone

stalagmite
stalagmiet, dripstone

stale
steil, oeld

stalk-1
(v-follow) staake

stalk-2
(e.g. plant) staak

stall-1
(stable, booth, stand) stal

stall-2
(v-delay) stalle

stamen
mieltred

stamina
outhoeldingsfermeyen, outlastingness

stammer
(n) stammer (v) stammere

stamp
(n-all meanings) stamp (v) stampe

stampede
(n) stampied, wildflyt (v) stampiede

stance
stand, hoelding

stand
(n) stand (v) stande

standby
(n) standby

stand by
(v) stande by

stand for
(v) stande for

stand-in
(n) stand-in

stand in
(v) stande in

stand in for
(v) stande in for

standing
(n) standing

stand-off
(n) stand-of

stand off
(v) stande av

standoffish
(adj) standoffish

standout
(n) standout

stand out
(v) stande out

standpoint
(n) standpunt

standstill
(n) standstil

stand up for
(v) stande up for

stand up to
(v) stande up tue

standard
standaard

standardization
normaliserring

standardize
normaliserrre

stanza
stanza

staple-1
(n-device) staapel (v) staapele

staple-2
(adj-regular stock) staapel (n) (regular stock) staapel

star
(n) staar, tungel (v) staare

starch
(n) staarch (v) staarche

stark
staark

starling
staarling

start
(n) staart (v) staarte

starter
staarter

starve
staarve, ferhungere

starvation
ferhungring

state
(n-condition) tuestand (n-pol.) staat (v) fercliere

statecraft
staatmanship, staatcraft

stateliness
staatligness

stately
staatlig

statesman
staatsman

statehouse
staathous

statement
cwyd, fercliering, geseyen

statesmanship
staatsmanship

statewide
staatwyd

static
(adj) stattish (n) aarbydsfermeyen

station
(n) stand, post; bus'halt, treinhalt (v) stasionerre, posterre

stationary
stilstand, stasionerr

stationery
letterpapier, wrytbehueften (pl)

Stations of the Cross
Belden av die Rued

statistical
statistish

statistician
statistiker

statistics
statistics

status
staat, posissen

statue
standbeld, onlykness

stature
gestalt

statute
statuet, laaw, wet

statutory
strafbaar

stay
(n) bly (vi, vt) blye, abyde

stead
sted

steadfast
stedfast

steadiness
steddigness

steady
steddig

steak
(cul) steik

steal
stiele

stealth
stelt

stealthy
steltig

steam
(n) stiem (v) stieme

steam bath
stiembat, souna

steamboat
stiemboet

steam engine
stiemmoeter

steamer
stiemer

steamship
stiemship

steamy
stiemig

steel
stiel

steel wool
stielwuel

steep -1
(adj) stiep

steep-2
(v) stiepe

steeple
stiepel

steer-1
(n-beef cattle) stier

steer-2
(v) stiere

steering wheel
stieringwiel

Stella
Stella

stem-1
(n-stalk) stem (v) stemme

stem-2
(v-stop) stemme

stench
stench

stencil
maarkplaat

step
(n) step (v) steppe

stepbrother
stepbrueder

stepchild
stepchild (-kind)

stepdaughter
stepdaater

stepfather
stepfaader

step down
steppe doun

Stephen
Steffen, Stievens

stepladder
stepladder

stepmother
stepmueder

stepparent
stepelder

stepping-stone
steppingstone

stepsister
stepsister

stepson
stepsoen

step up
steppe up

stereo
stereow

stereotype
(n) stereowtiep (v) stereowtiepe

sterile
steriel

sterilize

steriliserre

sterling
sterrling

stern-1
(adj) sterrn

stern-2
(nautical) sterrn

sternum
brestboen

steroid
sterroid

stethoscope
stettoscoep

Steven
Stieven
See Stephen

stew
(n) stuew (v) stuewe, stuewe about

stick
(n) stic (v) sticke

sticker
sticker

stick shift
sticshift

sticky
stickig

stiff
stif

stiffen
stiffene

stifle
smuedere

stifling
smuedrig

stigma
stigma

stigamatize
stigmatiserre

still
(adj) stil, stillig (v) stille; **be still** gestille, bie stil

stillbirth
stilburt

stillborn
stilborn

stilt
stilt

stilted
stilted

stimulant
upweikend middel, goeder, prodder, stimulanz

stimulate
goede, prodde, stimulerre

stimulation
stimulerring

sting
(n) sting (v) stinge

stink
(n) stink (v) stinke

stinky
stinking

stipend
setbetalling

stipulate
bedinge, stipulerre

stipulation
oeveryncuemst, stipulerring, aredness

stir
(n) stur (vi, vt) sturre

stir up
sturre up

stirrup
futhoeld

stitch
(n) stitch (v) stitche

stock
(n) stoc, foerraad (v) stocke

stockade
palisaad

stockbroker
stocbroeker, bursenmakler

stock exchange
burs

stockholder
bursbesitter

stocking
stocking

stole
did stiele

stomach
(n) maaw (v - **tolerate**) ferdragge

stock market
burs

stone
(n) stoen (v) stoene

stood
did stande

stool
(chair) stuel ; (bowel movement) defekerring

stoop-1
(n-porch-) stuep

stoop-2
(v) stuepe

stop
(n) stop, halt (v) stoppe, halte

storage
laagring, berrging

storehouse
heddern, laagerhous, werrhouse

storeroom
laagerruem, laagertimmer

stork
stork

storm
(n) storm, ist (v) storme

stormy
storming

story-1
teil, ferhaal

story-2
floer

storyteller
fertelling, ferhaaler

stout
stout, strang

stout-hearted
stouthaarted

stove
stoev

stow
stoewe

stowage
stoewen

stowaway
stoewawey

strafe
straafe

straggle
straggele

straggler
straggler

straight
streit

straighten
streitene

strain-1
(n-descent, lineage) strein, belasting

strain-2
(v) oeverspanne, belaste

strainer
fergiet, filter

strait
naarow waaterwey, waaterweylink

strand
strand

strange
fremd, od, maarkwurdig

stranger
fremder, fremdeling

strangle
detchoeke, worge

strangler
detchoeker, worger

strangulate
choeke av

strap
(n) strap (v) strappe

stratagem
plan, rench, tric, list

strategic
strateigish

strategist
strateigist, planner

strategy
strateigie

stratify
beleyere, forme leyers

stratosphere
stratosferr

stratum
leyer

stratus
cloudformaasen

straw
straaw

strawberry
straawberrie, errtberr

stray
(n) waanderdier (v) ferwaandere, ofwyke

streak
(n) striek (v) strieke

streaky
striekig

stream
striem

streamer
striemer

street
striet, lein

streetwalker
strietwaaker, strietfrouw, hoer

strength
strengt, myt

strengthen
strengtene, ferstrange, trimme

strenuous
aanstrengen, ennergish

stress
(n) betoening; (med) stres (v) betoene

stretch
(n) stretch (v) stretche

stretcher
stretcher

stretch out
stretche out, betenne

strew
struewe

stricken with (by)
stricken mid (by)

strict
streng, strict

stride
(n) stryd (v) stryde

strife
stryt, geflit, kies

strike
(n) stryk (v) stryke

strikeout
(n) strykout (v) stryke out

strikebreaker
strykbreiker

striker
stryker

string
(n) string (v) stringe

string up
stringe up

stringent
strict; (with money) tyt

strip-1
(n) strip (v) strippe

strip-2
(piece of something) strip

stripe
(n) stryp (v) strype

strive
spanne in self

strive agenst
stryde agenst

stroke
(n) stroke; (med) stroekfal (v) stroeke

stroll
(n) stroel (v) stroele

stroller
stroeler

strong
strang

strong-minded
strangminded

strong-willed
strangwild

structural
bouwlig

structure
bouw, structuer

struggle
(n) struggel (v) struggele

strum
(n) strum (v) strumme

strumpet
hoer, strietwaaker, strietfrouw

strut
(n) strut (v) strutte

strychnine
nytsheid, stricnien

stub
(n) stub (v) stubbe

stubby
stubbig

stucco
stuccow

stuck-up
stuc-up

stud-1
(board) stud

stud-2
(sexually active mare) stud

student
stuedent, lerrner

studio
stuediow

studious
yverig, stuedielienig, stuediebent

study
(n - room) stuedie (v) stuedie

stuff
(n) stuf (v) stuffe

stuffing
stuffing

stuffy
stuffig

stumble
(n) stumbel (v) stumbele, trippe

stump
(n) stump (v) stumpe

stun
oeveraawe, shocke, betoube

stunning
stunnish, ferbaazend, tol

stupendous
wuenderbaarlig, colosaal

stupid
dum, stom

stupidity
dumness, stomness

stupor
ferdoeving

sturdiness
stuerness

sturdy
strang, unyeldish, stuer

sty-1
(pigpen) sty

sty-2
(med) sty

style
(n) styl (v) stiliserre

stylish
moedish, swierig

stylist
styler

stylize
stiliserre

Styx
(myth) Stics

suave
gewand, frendlyk

sub-
(prefix) under-, sub-

subconscious
(adj) unawerr, underbewust (n) underbewust

subdivide
underferdiele

subdivision
underferdieling

subdue
underwerrpe, bedwinge

subject
(adj) underworpen; **subject to**- underworpen aan; **subject to the approval of**- behoelden av die welseying av (n) tiem (v) underwerrpe

subjunctive
subjunctive

sublet
underlette, underferhyere

sublime
subliem

submarine
undersieboet

submerge
(vi) touke; (vt) besinke, besenche

submission
underwerrping

submissive
underwerrpig

submit
(vt) underwerrpe, foerlegge (vi) underwerrpe self

subordinate
underling; (grammar) dependent

subpoena
(n) gerytsorder, deyvaarding (v) deyvaarde

subscribe
undertoekene; (to a magazine) abonerre

subscriber
undertoekner; (magazine) abonent

subscription
underwrit, abonement

subsequent
folgen

subside
lette up, wiekene

subsidiary
(adj) undergeshict (n) toctergeselshaft, undercompanie

subsidize
subvensionerre

substance
(n - essential part) edwist, essenz, weizen (physical matter) stuf, edwist

substantial
weisenlig, mutch, mennig

substantive
selfstandig wurd

substitute
(n) errsats (v) ferfange, teike die sted av, stande in for

subtenant
twiedhyerder, twiedmieter

subtract
teike awey (av), ferlessene

subtraction
weyteiking, ferlessning

suburb
foerstad, imstad

subway
underwey (-grund)

succeed
upfolge, faalowe, havve luc, spoewe

success
gued gefolg, luc, spoewness, sucses

successful
geluckig

succession
upfolging

successor
afterfolger, upfolger

such
sutch

suck
(n) suc (v) sucke

sucker
(candy) sucker (fool) sucker

suckle
suckele

Sudan
Sudaan

sudden
unfoersien, cwic, plotslig, breikend

Sue
(fem name) Sue

sue
(law) (vt) ferclagge (vi) clagge

sue for
fersieke im

suffer (from)
(vi) lyde aan; (vt) lyde

suffering
lyden

suffice
fulduewe, genuege

sufficient
fulduewend, genueg

suffix
wurdadder, afteradding

suffocate
fersticke

suffocation
fersticken

sugar
sueger

sugar diabetes

suegersicness

suggest
stelle foer

suggestion
taatgift, taatgeshenk, sugestie

suggestive
sugestiv

suicidal
selfkillish, selfmurdrish

suicide
selfkilling, selfmurder; (person) selfmurdernaar

suit
(n) (clothing) claddingset (cards) cloer (set)
(law) proses, laawcaas (v) passe

suitable
passend, behief, gedaffenlig

be suitable
gedaffene

sulfate
sulfaat, swaavel

sulfur
swaavel

sulk
(n) sulk (v) sulke

sullen
trist, souwer

sultan
sultan

sultry
sweltrish

sum
sum

sum up
summe up

+summa cum laude
mid hyest lof

summarize
resumerre

summary
sumier

summer
summer

summersoltice
summerstilstand, summersunhalt

summertime
summertyd

summit
top, hyest punt

summon
(v) (law) foerlaade; ruepe, calle fort

summons
calorder, bans

sun
sun

sun bath
sunbaat

sunbathe
sunbaade

sunbeam
sunstraal, sunbiem

sunburn
sunburn

sundae
sundie

Sunday
Sundey, Sundie

Sunday school
Kierkscuel

sunder
sunder

sundown
sundoun, sunset

sundry
sundrig

sunflower
sunbluem

sunglasses
sunglassen

sunless
sunless

sunrise
sunrys, sunup

sunshine
sunshyn

sunspot
sunspot

sunstroke
sunstroek

sunsuit
swimcladding

suntan
suntan, sunbrouning

sunup

sunup, sunrys

super
suepere, oever

super-
oever-

superior
best, hyest, greitest, fuldrish; **immediate superior** nierest hedman

superlative (degree)
oevertreffend trap; (adj) oevertreffelig

supermarket
suepermaarket

supernatural
oevernatuerlig

superstition
oevertrouw, bygeloef

superstitious
oevertrouwish, bygeloevig

supervise
waache oever, oeversie, sie tue

supervision
oeverwaach, oeversyt, tuesyt

supervisor
oeversieyer, oeverwaacher, inspector

supper
ievenmiel, ievenieten

supplement
(gen'l noun) suplement; (addition) tuesats
(newspaper) tueslaag (v) fille aan

supplier
bestaller

supplies
behoeldingen (-s)

supply
(n) leivering (v) leivere, fershaffe

support
(n) underhoeld (v) underholde, helpe, gefilste;
backe up (person)

supporter
underhoelder, backer, helper

suppose
ferunderstelle, fermuede

supposition
ferunderstelling

suppository
(med) supoesitor

suppress
drucke under (doun), ferbyte

suppression
ferbyting, bedrucking, underdrucking

supremacy
ferherrship, uppermyt, foerrang, eldership

supreme
hyest, oefrest

sure
secker, gladlig, gerrn

surely
secker, stellig

surf
(n) surf (v) surfe

surfing
surfen

surface
oeverflec, top (v) belegge, cueme aan die oeverflec, cueme tue die top, betoppe

surgeon
kirurg (col) hielercutter

surgery
kirurgie

surgical
kirurgish

surmount
oevercueme

surname
lastneim, kinneim

surpass
oevertreffe

surplus
oeverstoc, oevertelling

surprise
(n) ferrassing (v) ferasse

surprising
ferrassend

surrender
(n) oevergav (mil) capitulaasen, givve up (oever), (mil) capitulerre

surrogate
surogaat

surround
imringe, imsette, beferre

surroundings
imgivving, imweld

surveillance
oeverwaach

survey
(n) oeversyt, besting (v) lueke oever, oeversie besyte, (land) fermette

surveyor
landfermetter

survival
oeverlivven, (tradition) fortbestand

survive
(vt) oeverlivve (vi) livve aan, bestanne fort

survivor
oeverlivvender, aanlivvender

susceptible
fatbaar

susceptible to
fatbaar for

suspect
(n) ferdact (v) fertinke, ferdacte

suspend
calle av, halte, stoppe

suspense
spanning

suspension
uphanging

suspension-bridge
hangbridg

suspicion
fertinking, aftertaat

suspicious
ferdactig, mistrouwish

Swahili
Swahieli

swallow-1
(fowl) swaalow

swallow-2
(n) swaalow (v) swaalowe

swam
did swim

swamp
swamp

swap
(n) swaap (v) swaape

swarm
(n) swerrm (v) swerrme

swathe
sweide

sway
(n) swey (v) sweye

Swaziland
Swaaziland

swear
swerre

swear by
swerre by

swear in
swerre in

swear off
swerre av

sweat
(n) swet (v) swette

sweater
swetter, puloever

sweaty
swettig

swelter
sweltere

Swede
Swied

Sweden

Swieden

Swedish
Swiedish

sweep
(n) swiep (v) swiepe, feye

sweeper

swieper, feyer

sweepings
swiepingen (-s)

sweet
swiet, wierod

sweet corn
swietcorn

sweeten
swietene

sweetener
swietner

sweetheart
swiethaart

sweet pea
swietpie

sweet potato
swietpotaat

swell
(adj) swell (n) swell (v) swelle

swelling
swelling

swelter
sweltere

sweltering
sweltrig

swerve
(n) swerrv (v) swerrve

swift
swift

swill
(n) swil (v) swille

swim
(move through water) (n) swim (v) swimme

swimmingpool
swimpuel, swimbecken

swimsuit
swimshorts, baadanzug, swimcladddings

swindle
(n) swindel (v) swindele

swindler
swindler

swine
swyn, pig

swing
(n) swing (v) swinge

swing shift
swingshift

Swiss
(adj) Switsers (n - person) Switser (n-language)
Switserdutch

switche
(n) switch (v) switche

Switzerland
Switserland

swivel
(n) swivvel (v) swivvele

swivel chair
swivvelstuel

swollen
(perf. part. of **swell**) swoelen

sword
sord

swordfish
sordfish

swum
(perf. part. of **swim**) swum

swung
(pref. part of **swing**) swung

Sybil
(fem. name) Sibbil

Sydney
(masculine name) Sidni

syllable
wurdbreik, sillab

syllabus
lerrnplan

symbol
symbol

symbolic
simbollish

symbolism
simbolissem

symbolize
simboliserre

symmetry
simmetrie

sympathetic
simpatettish, midfielend

sympathize
midfiele, simpatiserre

sympathy
midfiel; (condolences) bylyden

symphonic
simfoenish

symphony
simfonie

symptom
simptom

symptomatic
simptomaatish

synagogue
sinnagoeg

synchronize
sincronisere

syndicate
(n) sindicaat (v) sindikerre

syndication
sindicaasen

synod
(rel) sinoed; kierkfergaddring

synonym
sinoniem

syntax
sintacsis

synthetic
syntettish

syphilis
siffilis

Syria
Siria

Syrian
(person) Sierie'en, Sierie'er (adj) Sieri'ish

syringe
sprits

syrup
sierup, swietwaater

system
sistem

systematic
sistemaatish

t

tab
ettiket, leibel

tabernacle
tabbernakel

table
taafel, ietbord, table

table spoon
taafelspuen

table wear
taafelwerr

taboo
tabuew

tabulate
tabulerre, nyme up in

tabulator
tabulator

tack
(n) tac (v) tacke (doun)

tackle
(n) tackel, teikdoun

taco
taacow

Tacoma
Tacoema

tact
tact

tactful
tactful

tactless
tactless

tag
(n) leibel, ettiket, tag

tail
teil

tailor
snyder

takeaway
(n) teikawey (v) teike awey

take back
(v) teike bac

takedown
(n) teikdoun

take down
(v) teike doun

takeoff
(n) teikof

take off
(v) teike av yn table

takeover
(n) teikoever

take over
teike oever

take prisoner
nyme gefangen

tale
teil

talent
tallent (v) tackele, teike doun

talented
tallented, tallentful

talk
(n) taak, spiech, sprec (v) taake, spieke, sprecke

talkback
(n) taakbac

talk back
(v) taake bac

talk over
(v) taake oever

talkative
taaksum, taakish (v) taage

tall
tal, hy

tallness
tallness, hyt

tallow
tallow

tally
(n) telling (v) telle

take
(n) teik (v) teike, nyme

talon
claw

tame
(adj) teim (v) teime

tan
(n) yellowbroun, tan

tandem
tandem

tang
tang

tangent
tangent

tangerine
mandarinappelsin, tangerien

tangible
graspbaar, gripbaar

tank
(gas recepticale) tank (military vehicle) tank

tantamount
belyk (tue)

tantalize
tantaliserre

tap-1
(n) (physical contact) tap, (v) tappe

tap-2
(n) (plumbing) tap (v) tappe

tape
(n) teip (v) teipe

tape measure
teipmet

tapeworm
teipwurm

taper
(n) teiper (v) teipere

tapir
taapier

Taps
(military) taps (v) tanne, tanninsoeke

tar
(n) taar (v) taare

tarantula
tarantulaw

tardiness
leitness

tardy
leit

target
(n) target (v) taargete

tariff
tarief

tarnish
(n) tarnish (v) taarnishe

tarpaulin
drynesskieper

tart-1
(adj) tart

tart-2
(n) (fruit pastry) taart

task
task, mustduew

taste
(n) smac (v) smacke

tasteful
smacful

tasteless
smacless

tasty
smaclig

tatoo
(n) tatuew (v) tatuewe

tattle
tattele

taut
taat (v) terre, rippe

tavern
inn

tax
(n) belasting (v) belaste, putte yn belasting
aan

taxation
belasting

tax-deductible
belastingferminderbaar

tax-exempt
belastingfrie

taxi
tacsie, taxi, cab

taxidermist
dierstuffer

taxidermy
dierstuffing

taxpayer
belastingbetaller

teammate
tiemmeit

teamwork
tiemwurk

tear-1 (rip)
(n) terr, rip

tear-2 (eyewater)
tier

teardrop
tierdrop

tearful
tierful

tease
tiese

teaspoon
teyspuen

technical
tecnish

technicality
tecnicaliteit

technician
tecniker

technique
tecniek

technologica
tecnoloegish

technologist
tecnoloeg

tea
tey

teabag
teybag

teach
tieche, belerrne

teacher
tiecher, belerrner

teaching
(profession) tieching, belerrning (act of)
tiechen, belerrnen

team
(n) tiem (vi, vt) tieme (up)

teapot
teypot

technology
tecnoloegie

tedious
langsum,langwylig

tee (golf)
tie

teem (with)
tieme (mid)

teen
tiener

teen-ager
tiener, tienyierling

teeth (pl. tooth)
tiet, tanden

telegram
tellegram

telegraph
(n) tellegraf (v) tellegraferre

telepathy
tellepatie

tendonitis
sinyuwswelling, sinyuwinflemming

telephone
(n) tellefoen (v) tellefoene, foene

telescope
tellescoep

telescopic
tellescoepish

televise
telleviserre

television
tellevissen

tell
telle

tell on
telle aan

tell off
telle av

teller
teller

telling
(adj) tellend

temper
temper

temperature
temperatuer

temperamental
temperamentel

tenacity
fasthoeldenness

Tenet
stelling

Tennessee
Tennesie

tennis
tennis

tenniscourt
tennisyaard, tennislaawn

tennis shoe
tennisshuew, snieker

tenor
tenoer, mellodiehoelder

tense-1
(gram) tyd

tense-2
gespand, taat, spannen

tension
spanning, taatness

tensor
stretchmuskel, stretchspier

tenant
hoelder, hyerder

tend
teike kerr av, waache oever

tent
telt, feldbed

tendency
liening, bentness

tender
tender, soft

tendon
sinyuw

tentacle
tentakel, fielorgaan

tentative
tentative, fornouwish

tenth
tent

tenuous
tin, slender, slyt

tenure
wurkryt

tepid
slytwaarm

term
terrm

terminable
endbaar

terminal
(adj) endish (n) endsted, endstaasen

terror
scric, frict

terrorism
scricness

terrorist
scricker, befricter

terrorize
terroriserre

tequila
tequila, tekielaw

test
(n) test, proeb (v) teste, proebe

testament
testament

testicle
secsclier, sexclier, begetclier, briedclier

terminate
ende. beende

termination
end, ending

termite
terrmiet, ryswurm

termless
terrmless

terrace
terras

terrestrial
(adj) errtig (n) errtbewoener

terrible
scriclig, grimlig, frecken

terrific
scriclig

terrify
ferscricke

territorial
territorial, gebiedish

territory
gebied

testify
bewyse, witnesse

testimonial
witnessing

testimony
witnessing

testosterone
manhormoen

Texas
Texas, Tecsas

text
text, tecst

textbook
textbuek, (tecst-)

textile
textiel (tecs-)

texture
textuer (tecs-)

Thai
(person/language) Ty

Thailand
Tyland

that
dat

there
derr

thaw
(n) taaw (v) taawe

the
die

theater
teater, pleyhous

theatrical
teatraalish

thee
die

theft
teft

their
derr

theirs
derrs

theism
godbelief

them
dem

theme
teim, teima

themselves
demselven

theocracy
godregerring

Theodore
Teodoer

theologian
teoloeg

theology
teoloegie

theory
teorie

theosophie
teosoefie

therapist
terraper

therapy
terrapie

thermometer
terrmometter

thermostat
terrmostaat

these
dies

thesis
stelling, teisis, disertaasen, pruefwrit

they
dey

thick
tic

thicken
tickene

thickness
ticness

thief
tief

thigh
ty

thimble
finggerhat

thin
tin

thine
dyn

thing
ting

think
tinke

think of
tinke av

think over
tinke oever

thinness
tinness

third
dierd

thirst
turst

thirteen
diertien

thirtieth
diertiget

thirty
diertig

this
dis

thistle
tissel

Thomas
Tommas, Tomaas

Thor (myth)
Toer

thorax
chest

thorn
torn

thrash
trashe

thrash out
trashe out

thrash over
trashe oever

thread
(n) tred (vi, vt) tredde

threat
tret

threaten
trettene

three
drie

threw (pt. of throw)
did troewe

thrift
trift

thrifty
triftig

thrill
(n) tril (v) trille

thriller
triller

thorny
tornig

thorough
torro

thoroughfare
torroferr

those
does

thou
dou

though
doe

thought (pt. of think)
did tinke

thought
(n) taat

thoughtful
taatful

thoughtless
taatless

thousand
tousend

thrall
tral, wyvel, slaav

thralldom
traldum, wyveldum, slaaverny

throat
troet

throb
(n) troeb (v) troebe

throe(s)
troe(s)

throne
troen

throng
(n) trong, croud (v) tronge, croude

Through
Dur

Throughout
duroever

throughway
spiedwey, hywey, friewey

throw
(n) troew,worp (v) troewe, werpe

throwaway
(n) troewawey

throw away
(v) troewe awey

throwback
(n/adj) troewbac

throw back
(v) troewe bac

throw up
(v) troewe up

thrust
(n) trust (v) truste

thud
(n) tud (v) tudd

thumb
tum

thunder
(n) tunder (v) tundere

Thunderbolt
tunderboelt

Thursday
Toersdey

thus
dus

thwart
twaarte

thy
dy

thyroid
sheldclier, tieroid

Tibet
Tibet

tibia
shinboen, tiebie

tick-1 (sound)
(n) tic (v) ticke

tick-2 (zoolology)
tic

ticket
(n) ticket (v) tickete

tickle
(n) tickle (v) tickele

ticklish
ticlish

tidal
tydish

tide
(n) tyd (v) tyde

tidy
tydig

tie
(n) ty (v) tye, tye up

tier
leyer

tiger
tieger

tight
tyt

tighten
tytene, fertyte

till-1 (conjunction)
til, until

tip-3 (hint)
tip

till-2 (agriculture)
tille

tip-off
tipof

till-3 (drawer)
til

tipsy
tipsig

tillage
landtilling

tiptoe
(n) tiptoe (v) tiptoewe

tilte
tilte

timber
(adj/n) timber

tirade
tiraad

time (hour)
(n) tyd; (number of) (n) tym (v) tyde, tyme

tire-1 (fatigue)
(v) tyere

tire-2 (pneumatic)
(n) tyer

tiresome
tyersum

timekeeper
tydkieper, tymkieper

tissue
tissuw

tit (anatomy)
tit, tiet

timeless
tydless

titanium
titaanium

timid
shy

tithe
(rel.) (v) tyde

Timothy
Timmoti

title
(n) tietel, beneiming (v) tietele, beneime

tin
tin

tin can
tincan

to
tue

tine
tyn

toad
toed

tingle
(n) tingel (v) tingele

toast-1 (culinary)
(n) toest (v) toeste

tiny
tynig

toast-2 (honor)
(n) toest (v) toeste

tip-1 (pointed end)
tip

tip-2 (tip over)
tippe

tobacco
tabaak

today
tuedey

tombstone
greivstoen

toe
(n) toew (v) toewe

tomorrow
tuemorgen

ton
tun

toehold
toewhoeld

tone
(n) toen (v) toene

toenail
toewneil

together
tuegedder

tounge
(n) tung (v) tunge

toil
wurke haard

toilet
toilet

tonight
tuenyt

toiletpaper
toiletpapier

tonsil
mangel

token
toeken

too
tue

told (pt. of tell)
did telle

tool
tuel

tolerable
berrbaar

toot
(n) tuet (v) tuete

tolerance
toleranz

tolerant
berrbaar

top-1 (highest point)
(adj/n) top

tolerate
tolererre, berre, putte up mid

top-2 (toy)
top

topic
underwerrp, teima

toleration
ferberring

toll-1 (tax)
toel

topical
actuwel

toll-2 (ring)
(n) toel (v) toele

topology
topoloegie

topping
topping

tomato
tomaat

topple
toppele

tomb
greiv

torch
(n) fackel (v) befackele

touching
beruerend

tore (past tense of tear)
did terre

touchy
liggeraak

torment
(n) foltring, tinter (v) foltere, tintere

tough
tuf

toughen
tuffene

tormenting
tinterlig

tour
(n) ress, tuer, imgang (v) tuere

tornado
twister, tornaadow, wurlwind

tourism
tuerissem

torpedo
(n) torpeidow (v) torpederre

tourist
tuerist

tournament
turnier

torso
torsow

tourniquet
twistband

tortuous
twistful, turnful, windig

tow
(n) toew (v) toewe

torture
(n) folter, tinter (v) foltere, tintere

towel
dryclot, wypclot

tower
(n) touwer (v) touwere

torturer
folteraar

toss
(n) tos (v) tosse

town
toun, stad

township
tounship

total
(n) totaal (v) totaale, beloepe

toxic
giftig, toxic, tocsic

toxicologist
toxicoloeg (tocs-)

totalitarian
totaliterr, giftkenner

touch
(n) beruering, (v) beruere

toxicology
giftloer, toxicoloegie (tocs-)

traitor
ferraader

toxin
giftstuf, toxin (tocs-)

tramp
tramp

toy
(n) toy (v) toye mid

trample
trampele

trampoline
trampolien

trace
(n) maark, spuer (v) draawe, outlyne

trance
tranz

tranquil
calm, ruewig, stillig

trachea
lungpyp

track
(n) (fuet)spuer (-maark) (v) faalowe (folge)
spuer

trans-
oever-

transact
ferhandele

tract
pamflet, tract

transaction
ferhandling

traction
trecking, grip

transcontinental-

transcontinentaal

trade
(n) treid; (occupation) bedrift (v) treide

transcript
oeverwrit

trade-in
treid-in

transfer
(n) fersetting (v) fersette, hande oever
oeversende

trademark
treidmaark

trade wind
treidwind

tradition
tradissen

transference
oeversending

traditional
tradissionaal

transform
ferforme, ferandere

trail
(n) fuetpat (v) faalowe, folge

transformation
ferforming, ferandring

train
(n) trein (v) getiete

transformer
transformaator

transfuse
(med) instille

transportation
transport, transportaasen

transfusion
instilling, transfuesen

transsexual
transsexuaal, transsecsuaal, sexferandringer,
secsferandringer

transgress
laawbreike, sinne

transgression
laawbreiking, sin

transvestite
oevercladder

trap
(n) trap (v) trappe

transit
duergang

transition
ferandring

trapeze
trapeiz

transitive
(gram) transitive

trash
(n) trash (v) trashe

translate
fertaale, oeversette

translation
fertaaling , oeversetting

travel
(n) res, weyferr (v) resse, weyferre

translator
fertaaler, oeversetter

transmigrate
(rel) ferhouse

travel agency
resagensie

transmigration
ferhousing

travel agent
resagent, resbehandler

transmission
oeversending, fortsending

tray
trey

transmit
oeversende, fortsende

treacherous
ferraadelig

transmitter
fersender

treachery
ferraad

transparent
duersytig

tread
(n) tred (v) tredde

transplant
ferplante

transport
(n) transport (v) transporterre

treason
ferraad, beswyk, bewreying

treasonable
beswyig

treasure
(n) hord, scat (v) horde, hoelde in erren

treasurer
hordkieper, scatkieper

treasury
hordkammer, scatkammer

treat
(n) triet (v) behandele

treatment
behandling

treaty
ferdrag

tree
(n) trie (v) trie

trek
(n) trec (v) trecke

trellis
trellis

tremble
(n) shudder (v) shuddere, cweike, siddere

tremendous
ferscric, gewaltig

tremor
cweik, siddring

trench
ditch

trend
(n) trend (v) trende

trendy
trending

trespass
(n) oevergang (v) oevergoewe

trey
trey

tri- (prefix)
tri-, drie-

triage (medical)
behandlingorder

trial
ferhiering

triangle
driehuek

triangular
driehuekig

tribal
clan- (combining form); clannish

tribe
clan

tribulation
(rel) ferdrucking, tribulaasen

tribunal
geryts'hof

tribute
(tax) scatting (honor) err

triceps
triseps

trick
(n) tric (v) tricke

trickery
trickerie

tricky
trickig

trickle
(n) trickel (v) trickele

triplet
drieling

tricycle
driewieler

trifle
(n) clyniger (v) behandele lytlig mid

trifling
fickel

trigger
(n) trigger (v) triggere

trigonometry
trigonoemetrie

trilateral
driesydig

trilogy
triloegie

trim
(n) trim (v) trimme

trimester
trimester

trimming
trimming

trinity
drieynness; (rel) Hoelig Drieynness

trio
triow

trip
(n) trip (v) trippe

triple
(adj) driefoldig (n) driebaager (v) ferdriefoldige

triplet
drieling

triplicate
driefoldig, triplicaat

triumph
(n) triomf (v) triomferre

triumphal
triomfig

trivia
belanglessing

trivial
belangless

troop
(n) truep (v) truepe

trooper
trueper

trophy
wintoeken, troefie

tropic
troepish

tropics
troepen

trot
(n) trot (v) trotte

trouble
(n) fertriet, woew (v) fertriete

troublemaker
fertrietmeiker

troubleshooter
fertrietshueter

troublesome
fertrietsum

trough
troef

trousers
trousers

trout
trout

trow
believe, tinke, troewe

trowel
troffel

truce
trues

truck
(n) truc (v) trucke

true
truew, waar

truly
truewlig

trumpet
(n) trompet (v) trompeterre

trunk
trunk; (for traveling) coffer

trust
(n) trust (v) truste

trustee
trustie

trustful
trustful

truth
truet, waarness

truthful
truetful, betroewbaar

try
(n) proeb, fand (v) proberre, fande

try on
befande

tryout
(n) ferhiering (v) ferhiere

trying
shwierig

tsar
kyser

tub
tub

tuba
tueba

tube
pyp

tuberculosis
terring, lungsicness

tubing
pyping

tuck
(n) tuc (v) tucke

Tuesday
Tuesdey

tug
(n) tug (v) tugge

tuition
underryt, tuissen

tulip
tulp

tumble
(n) tumbel (v) tumbele

tumor
swelling, tuemor

tuna
tuena

tune
(n) tuen, mellodie (v) tuene

tuneup
(n) tuenup

tune up
(v) tuene up

tunnel
(n) tunnel (v) tunnele

turn
(n) turn (v) turne

turncoat
turncoat

turn down
turne doun

turnip
raap

turnoff
(n) turnof

turn off
(v) turne av

turn on
(v) turne aan

turnout
(n) turnout

turnover
(n) turnoever

turn over
(v) turne oever

turnpike
turnpyk

turn up
(v) turne up

turpentine
turpentine

turret
turmken

turtle
turtel, siesheldtoed

tusk
tusk

tutor
privaattiecher, tuetor

tutorial
tutorrish

tuxedo
tuxeidow (tucs-)

twang
twang

tweak
(n) twiek (v) twieke

tweezers
twiezers

twelfth
twelft

twelve
twelv

twentieth
twentiget

twenty
twentig

twice
twys

twilight
twylyt

twin
twin, twilling

twine
(n) twyn (v) twyne

twinge
(n) twing (v) twinge

twinkling
twinkling

twist
(n) twist (v) twiste

twitch
(n) twitch (v) twitche

two
twie

two-faced
twie-ansyted, fals

twosome
twiesum

tydings
tydingen, tydings

tympanic membrane
ierdrum

tympanum
middelier

type
(n) tiep, sort, kind (v) tiepe

ty pewriter
tiepwryter, scribmashien

typical
tiepish

typhoid
tiefoid

tyrannical
tirannish

tyrannize
tiranniserre

tyranny
tirannie

tyrant
tiran

u

udder
udder

Uganda
Uganda

ugliness
ugligness, hesligness

ugly
uglig, heslig

Ukraine
Ucrein

Ukrainian
(adj) Ucreinish (n-person, language) Ucreinish

ukulele
uculeiley, ukulele

ulcer
swerr

ulcerate
swerre

ulcerous
swerrish

ulna
ulna

ulterior
hidden, gehym

ultimate
outerst, beslissend

ultimatum
endbeslyt, ultimaatum

umbrella
reinsheld, sunsheld

umlaut
umlout

umpire
shiedsryter

unabated
unferminderd

unable
unbecwaam

unacceptable
unaannymlig

unaccompanied
alyn

unaccustomed
ungewoen

unanimous
ynstemmig, ynmindish

unanimity
ynstemmigness

unarmed
unbeweppend

unashamed
unasheimd

unassuming
stilferrig

unaware
unawerr

unawares
unawerrs

unbearable
unberrbaar

unbeatable
unoeverwinnish

unbecoming
unbetaamlig

unbelief
unbelief

unbelievable
unbelievbaar

unbending
unbending

unbiased
unpartyig, ferr

uncertain
unsecker, feranderlig

uncle
onkel, faadersbrueder, muedersbrueder

uncommon
ungewoen

unconscionable
unbesheimd

unconscious
unawerr, unbewust

unconstitutional
unconstitusionel

uncontrollable
unbedwingbaar

undecided
unbeslis, beslytless

undependable
unfertrouwbaar

under
under

underclothes
undercladdings

undergo
undergoewe

undergraduate
underdiploemhoelder

underline
understryke, underlyne

underling
underling

underneath
underniet

understand
understande ferstande

understandable
understandbaar, ferstandbaar

undertake
underteike, undernyme

undertaker
underteiker, belykhandler

undertaking
underteiking, undernyming

underworld
underweld

underwrite
underwryte

undo
unduewe

undoing
unduewing

undoubtedly
untwyvelig, sonder twyvel

undress
uncladde (self)

undying
undyig

unemployable
unferhyerbaar

unemployed
unferhyerd, workless, aarbydless

unequal
ungelyk

unfair
unferr, unryt

unfinished
unfulended

unfit
unfit, ungeshic

unfold
unfoelde

unfriendly
unfrendlig

ungodly
ungodlig

unhappy
unhappig

unhindered
unhindered

unholy
unhoelig

uniform
uniform, lykcladding

unimportant
unbelangrig, unwictig

unintelligible
unferstandbaar

union
feryniging

unique
ynig

unit
ynness; (math) yner

unite
ferynige

unity
ynness, ferbond

United Kingdom
Ferynigd Kingdum

United States
Ferynigd Staats

universal
algemein

universe
univerrs

unlucky
unluclig

unmarried
unwedded

unmistakable
unmisteikbaar, secker

university
univerrsiteit

Unitarian
Unitaar, Teigendrie-ynnesser

unjust
unferr, unryt

unkind
unkind, unfrendlig

unknown
unbekend

unlawfulness
unlaawful, unwettig

unless
unless

unlike
un(ge)lyk

unlikely
un(ge)lyklig

unload
unloede

unlock
unlocke

unnatural
unnatuerlig

unnecessary
unnotwendig

unoccupied
unbeset, unbewoen

unofficial
unofissi'el

unpardonable
unfergivbaar

unpack
unpacke

unpleasant
(things) unaangenaam; (people) unwinsum

unpopular
unpopulerr

unprofessional
unprofessionaal

unpromising
ungunstig

unreal
unwurklig

unreasonable
unreidelig

unreliable
unbetrouwbaar

unrest
unrest

unrighteous
unrytish

unripe
unryp

unruly
unruewlig

unsociable
ungezellig

up
up

upbringing
upbringing

uphold
uphoeld

upkeep
upkeep

upon
upaan

upper
upper **Upper House**- Upper Hous

upright
upryt

uprising
uprysing

upset
(n) upset (v) upsette

upstairs
upsterrs

upstanding
upstandig

upswing
upswing

uptown
uptoun

upturn
upturn

uranium
uraan

urethra
urettra

urge
(n) aandrang (v) aandringe

urgent
dringend

urgency
dringendness

urinal
pisboel, urinal

urine
pis, urine

Uruguay
Urugwy

unseasonable
untydlig

unselfish
unselfish

unskilled
unskild

unsteady
unsteddig, feranderlig

untenable
unferdeddigbaar, unhoeldbaar

unthankful
untankful

unthinkable
untinkbaar

untie
untye

until
until

untold
untoeld

untoward
untuewaard

untrue
untruew, fals

unusual
ungewoen

unwholesome
unhoelsum, ungesund

unwilling
unwillig

unworthy
unwurdig

us
us

use
(n) gebruek, benutsing, ferwending (v)
benutse, ferwende

useful
nutsig, bruekbaar, dienstig

useless
nutsigless

user
gebrueker, benutser

usher
stedaaanwyser

usual
gewoenlig, gebrueklig

Utah
Uetaaw

uterus
ueterus

utility
nutsigness

utter
uttere

uvula
uevula

Uzbekistan
Uzbeikistaan

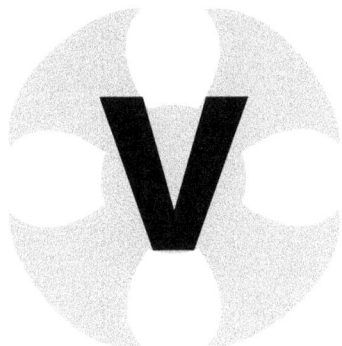

V

vacancy
emptigness, factuer

vacant
emptig, frie, facant

vacate
emptige, facterre

vacation
frietyd, wurkfrietyd, ferri'en

vaccinate
inente, vacsinerre

vaccination
inenting, vacsinerring

vacuum
(n) vaacum (v) vacumerre

vagina
vagiena

vagrant
tramp, landloeper

vague
unsecker, cloudig

vain
ydel, fergeblig

valid
geldig

validity
geldigness

valley
daal

valuable
wurdful, costbaar

value
(n) wurt (v) sette wurt

vandalism
vandalissem

vane
faan, vaan

vanilla
vanilla

vanish
ferswinde

vanquish
oeverwelme, oeverwinne

vapor
damp, stiem

vaporize
ferdampe, ferstieme

vaporizer
ferdamper, ferstiemer

variable
(n) variabel (adj) ferandrig

variation
ferandring

variety
fershiedenness

various
fershieden, fershillend, missenlitch

vary
ferandere, fershille

vascular
vascular

vase
vaas

vast
wyd

vat
vat

Vatican
Vaticaan

vault-1
(n) seckernessruem

vault-2
(v) springe, liepe

veal
caafflesh, calfflesh

vegetables
grienten

vegetarian
(adj) vegetaarish (n) vegetaari'er, grientenieter

vegetation
plantlyf

vehicle
ferbeweyer

veil
(n) slyer (v) ferslyere

vein
adder

vending machine
fercuepatomaat

vendor
fercueper

venerable
oerwurdig

vengeance
wraak

vengeful
wraakbent, wraaklienig

venial
ferclynbaar, fergivbaar

venison
haartflesh

venom
fergift, ettren

venomous
fergiftig

vent
(n) oepning (v) feroepene

versus
agenst

ventilate
ventilerre

ventilation
ventilerring

ventilator
ventilaator

ventricle
haartcammer

Venus (myth)
Venus (astrological)
Venus

veranda
veranda

verb (gram)
wurkwurd, verrb

verbal
wurkwurdig, verrbaal

verbatim
wurd for wurd

verdict
oerdiel, beslis

verge
edg, brink

verification
becraftiging, betruetiging

verify
becraftige, verriferre

Vermont
Verrmont

vernacular
foelktaal

verse
ferrs, verrs

versify
beferrse

verson
oeversetting, fertaaling

vertical
verrticaal

vertigo
swindle

very
(intens.) bissen, soer, radder, prettig, wurklig

Vespers
ievensang, ievningebed

vessel
(container) behoelder (seacraft) ship

vest
vest, Vesta (myth), Vesta

vestibule
inweyhal,inganghal

veteran
veteraan

veterinarian
dierloeker

veterinary
dierloekish

vex
beswenche

via
via, by

viaduct
viaduct

vial
flask

vibrate
vibrerre, cwivvere

vibration
vibrerring, cwivvring

vicar
vicker

**vice- under-
vice**
untie, vies, laster

vicinity
neiberhued, nierness

vicious
wicked, ievil

victim
opferling

victimize
shicanerre

victor
sieger, oeverwinner

victorious
siegrig, oeverwinnish

victory
sieg, oeverwin

video
video

view
(n) gesyt (v) besytige, **point of view**-
gesytpunt

vigilant
waachful, kerrful

Viking
Vieking

village
torp, hamling, buerow

Vincent (masculine name)
Vinsent

vine
wynstoc

vinegar
essig

vineyard
wynyaard

violate
ferletse, fercrafte
violation ferletsing, fercrafting

violator
ferletsinger, fercrafter

violence
heftigness

violent
heftig

violin
fiddel, violin

viper
adder

Virgil
(masculine name)
Virgil

Virgin
meiden

virile
manlig

virtue
befastness, oerfastness

virus
virus

visa
visum, ingangliev
visible
sytbaar

visualize
visualiserre

visibility
sytbaarness

vision
(something seen) vissen; (ability to see) siemyt,
sytmyt

visit
(n) besiek (v) besieke

visitor
besieker

visor
ygersheld, ygersheid

visual
(adj/n) visu'el

Vista
vista, outsyt

vital
(comb. form) lyf-; lyfwictig

vitamin
vitamin

Vivian (fem name)
Viviaan

vocabulary
wordlist, wurdstoc

vocal
(adj) stemmig; (n) sang

vocal cord
stemband

vocalist
singer

vodka
vodka

voice
(n) stem (v) bestemme

Voiced
stemhavvend

voiceless
stemless

volt
volt

voltage
(striem)spanning

volume
voluem, set

voluntarily
friewillig,selfwillig, willig

volunteer
friewilliger
vomit (n) voemit , troewup (v) voemite,
troewe up

vote
(n) stem (v) stemme

voter
stemmer

vow
(n) beloft (v) believe

vowel
clinker, vocaal

voyage
trip

vulgar
bewoen, ordinerr

vulgarity
foelksprec, loewsprec

vulnerable
ferwundbaar

vulture
gyer, dedfleshfrieter

W

wade
weide

waffle
waffel

wag
(n) waag (v) wage

wage
wurkgeld, aarbydgeld

wagon
waagen

waist
weist

wait
(n) weit, abyde (v) weite

waiter
weiter, kelner

wait for
weite for

waitingroom
weitruem, weittimmer

waitress
waitress, kelnerin

wait on
weite aan

wait up

weite up

wake
(vt) weike

wake up
(vi, vt) weike up

walk
(n) waak, stroel, (v) waake, goewe for yn waak, teike yn waak

wall
wal

wall in
walle in

walnut
walnut

walrus
walrus

waltz

(n) wals (v) walse

wander
waandere

wander about (around)
waandere about(imber)

want (n) (lack)
want, lac, mangel

want (v)
wille tue + infinitive, ferlange

wanton
wanten

war
crieg, hild, saccuw, goud

make war
meike hild, behilde

warden
worden

ware (s)
werr (s)

warehouse
werrhous

wariness
werriness, spatsiergang

warlock
werrlaak

warlord
crieglord

warm
waarm

warmth
waarmt

warn
waarne

warning
waarning

warrant
(n) fulmytpapier (v) berytige, rytshoewe

Warrior
kemper, crieger, hilderink, wyger, soldaat, sedg

wary
werrig

was (pt of be)
did bie

wash
(n) wash, washing (v) washe

washing machine
washmashien

Washington (city/state)
Washington

Wasp
wasp

Waste
(n) swil, offel, fercwisting, misspending,
misbruek (v) fercwiste, misspende, misbrueke

waste away
ferdwyne

watch (n)
waach (v) waache

watch over
waache oever, bewerre

water
(n) waater (v) waatere

watercraft
watercraft

waterfall
waaterfal

watermelon
waatermeloen

watery
waatrig

wave
(n) weiv (v) weive

waver
(n) weiver (v) weivere

wax
(n) wax, wacs (v) waxe, wacse, fergreite

wax paper
waxpapier (wacs-)

way
wey

wayfarer
weyferrder

waylay
weyleye

Wayne (masc name)
Wein

Way of the Cross
Wey av die Cros

we
wie

weak
wiek, untrum, swac

weaken
wiekene, ferswacke

wealth
welt, ritchness

wealthy
weltig

wean
wiene

weapon
weppen

weaponry
weppenrie

wear
(n) werr (v) werre

wear out
werre out

wearable
werrbaar

wearing
werrend

wearisome
wierisum

weary
wierig

weasand (anatomy - esophagus)
wiesend

weasel
wiesel

weather
(n) wedder (v) weddere

weatherman
wedderreporter, climatoleg

weave
(n) wiev (v) wieve

web
(n) web (v) webbe

webbing
webbing

wed
wedde

wedded
wedded

wedding
wedding

wedlock
wedlock

Wednesday
Woedensdey

wedge
(n) wedg (v) wedge

wee
(adj) wie

weed
(n) wied (v) wiede

weedy
wiedig

week
wiek

weekday
wiekdey

weekend
weekend

weekly
wieklig

ween (suppose)
wiene

weep
wiepe

weeping
(adj) wiepend

weepy
wiepig

weigh
(vi, vt) weye

weight
weit, wect

weighty
weitig, wectig

weird
wierd

welcome
(n/adj) welcuem (v) welcueme

wellhead
(source) welhed

well-off
wel-of

well spring (full supply)
welspring

wend
wende

went (past tense of go)
did goewe

wept (pt of weep)
did wiepe

west
west

westerly
westerlig

western
western

wet
(adj/n) wet, nat (v) wette

wetland(s)
wetland(s)

whale
(n) weil (v) weile

wharf
worf, ky

wheat
wiet

wheedle
wiedele

wheel
(n) wiel (v) wiele

wheelbarrow
wielbaarow

wheeze
(n) wiez (v) wieze

wheezy
wiezig

when
wen

whence
wenz

whenever
wenevver

where
werr

whereabouts
werrabouts

wherever
werrevver

wherewithal
werrmidal

which
witch

while
wyl

whim
wim

whine
(n) wyn (v) wyne

whip
(n) wip (v) wipe

whiplash
whiplash

whipped cream
wipt criem

whirl
(n) wurl (v) wurle

whisker(s)
wisker(s)

whiskey
wiskie

whisper
(n) wisper (v) wispere

whistle
(n) wissel (v) wissele

white
wyt

whiten
wytene

whiteout

(n) wytout

white out
(v) wyte out

Whitsunday
Wytsundey

Whitsuntide
Wytsuntyd

whittle
wittele

who
hue

whoever
hue'evver

whole (entire)
hoel (healthy) heltig, gesund (complete)
fulstandig, fulcuemen

wholesale
hoelseil

wholesome
hoelsum

wholly
hoellig

whom
huem

whore
(n) hoer (v) hoere

whose
hues

why
wy

wicked

wicked

wicket
wicket

wide
wyd

widen
wydene

width

widt

widow
widow

widower
widower

wield
wielde

wife
wyf, frouw

wiggle
(n) wiggel (v) wiggele

Wilbur (masculine name)
Wilber

wild
wild

wilderness
wilderness

wildlife
wildlyf

Wilfred (Wilfrid) (masculine name)
Wildred

will-1 (modal auxillary)
wil

will-2 (decree)
wil, besetness

William (masculine name)
Willem

willing
(ge) willig, willend

willingly
willendlig

willow
willow

wilt
wilte

win
(n) win, oeverwinning (v) winne, oeverwinne

wind-1 (air current)
wind

wind-2 (turn)
winde

windmill
windmil

window
window, fenster

windpipe
windpyp

windup
(n) windup

wind up
(v) winde up

windy
windig

wine
wyn

wing
(n) wing (v) winge

wink
(n) wink (v) winke

winnings
winningen(-s)

winsome
winsum

winter
(n) winter (v) wintere

winterize
winteriserre

winter solstice
wintersunstilstand

wintertime
wintertyd

wintry
wintrig

wipe
(n) wyp (v) wype

wire
(n) wyer (v) wyere

wiring
wyring

Wisconsin
Wisconsin

wisdom
wisdom

wisdom
wisdom

wise
wys

wisent
wiesent

wish
(n) wish (v) wishe

wishful
wishful

wit
witte

witch
witch

witchcraft
witchcraft

with
mid

with-
(prefix) wid-

withdraw
widdraawe

withdrawal
widdraawel

wither

widdere

withhold
widhoelde

within
binnen

without
sonder

withstand
widstande

witless
witless

witness
(n) witnes (v) witnesse

-witted (suffix)
-witted

witticism
wittiling

witting
wittend

witty
wittig

wizard
wizzerd

wizen
wiezen

Woden

(myth) Woeden

woe
woew

woeful
woewful

wolf
wulf

wolverine
wolverien

woman
frouw

womanhood
frouwhued

womanly
frouwlig

won (past tense of win)
did winne

wonder
(n) wunder, wunderwurk (v) wundere

wonderful
wunderful

wonderland
wunderland

wonderwork
wunderwurk

wonderworking
wunderwurkend

wondrous
wundrig

won't
willnie, will nit

woo
wuewe

wood
wued, holt

woodchuck
wuedchuc

wooden
wueden

woodpecker
wuedpecker

woods
wueds

woodwork
wuedwurk

wool
wul

woolen
wullen

woolly
wullig

word
(n) wurd (v) wurde

wordbook
wurdbuek

wording
wurding

wordy
wurdig

work
(n) wurk, aarbyd (v) wurke, aarbyde

workable
wurkbaar, aarbydbaar

workaholic
wurkbenter, aarbydbenter

worker
wurker, aarbyder

world
weld

worldly
weldlig

worm
wurm

wornout
wornout

worrisome
wurrisum

worry
(n) wurrie (v) wurrie

worse
wurs

worsen
wursene

worship
(n) wurship , feroer (v) wurshipe, feroere

worst
wurst

worth
wurt

worthless
wurtless

worthwhile
wurtwyl

worthy
wurdig

would
(modal aux) wud

wound
(n) wuend (v) wuende

wrap
(n) wrap (v) wrappe

wrapping
wrapping

wrap-up
(n) wrap-up

wrap up
(v) wrappe up

wrath
wraat

wrathful
wraatful

wreak
wrieke

wreath
wriet

wreathe
wriede

wreck
(n) wrec (v) wrecke

wreckage
wrectyl

wrecker
wrecker

wren
wren

wrench
wrench, spanner

wrest
wreste

wrestle
(n) wressel (v) wressele (v - colloquial) ressele

wriggle
(n) wriggel (v) wriggele

wring
(n) wring (v) wringe

wringer
wringer

wrinkle

(n) wrinkel (v) wrinkele

wrist
wrist

wristband
wristband

wristwatch
wristwaach

writ
writ

write
wryte

write down
wryte doun

writer
wryter

writeoff
(n) wrytof (v) wryte av

write out
wryte out

write-up
(n) wryt-up

write up
(v) wryte up

writhe
wryde

wrong
(adj) wrang, unryt (n) wrang (v) wrange

wrongdoing
wrangduewing

wrongful
wrangful

wry
wry

wurst (culinary)
wurst

Wyatt (masculine name)
Wyet

Wyoming
Wyoeming

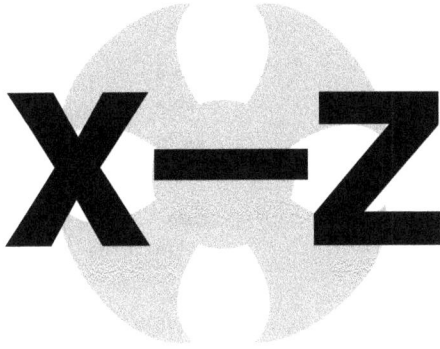

X–Z

xylophone
zielofoen

x-ray
(n) x-ray (n) x-straal (v) behandele mid
x-straals

-y
(adj-sfx) -ig

yacht
yaat, genuegenboet

yam
yam

yank
(n) yank (v) yanke

yard -1
(measure tool) yaard

yard-2
(lawn) yaard

yarn
yaarn

Yaweh
Yaawey

yawn
(n) yaan (v) yaaane

yearly
yierlig

yearn
yierne

yearning
yierning

yeast
yiest

yell
(n) yel (v) yelle

yellow
yellow

yellow fever
yellowfieber

yellow jacket
yellowwasp

yardstick
yaardstic

year
yier

yes
yaa

yester
(adj) yester

yesterday
yesterdey

yet
yet

yearbook
yierbuek

yield
(n) yeld (v) yelde, givve in (up)

yodel
(n) yoedel (v) yoedele

yoga
yoega

your
yor

yogurt
yoegert

yoke
(n) yoek (v) yoeke

yonder
yonder

you
yue

Yugoslavia
Yugoslaavie

young
yung

youngster
youngster

yours
yors

youth (individual)
yungen; yunghued, yungtyd

Yugoslavic
Yugoslaavic

yule
yuel

yuletide
yueltyd

Zaire
Zaa'ier

Zambia
Zaambie

zeal
iever, wilm, anter

zealot
iefriger

zealous
iefrig

zebra
ziebra

zenith
zienit

zero
(adj/n) zierow

Zeus
(myth) Zues

zinc
zink

Zionism
Zie'onissem

zip
(n) zip (v) zippe

zodiac
zoediac

zonal
zoenig

zone
zoen

zoo
diertyn, zoew

zoological
zoewloegish

zoologist
zoewloeg

zucchini
zukienie

JOHN C. RICKER

A Portrait Gallery

Burton, Ohio, circa 1953

Burton, Ohio, 1953
[PHOTO BY JOHN'S SISTER, SHIRLEY SHEFCHUK]

U.S. Airman Basic 1955–1959
Parks Air Force Base near Oakland, California

Burton High School Class of 1955,
Ohio University 1962, Bowling Green University 1970

Chardon High School 1962–63,
Jefferson High School 1963–1996

John C. Ricker and Emily F. Carroll
June 3, 1967
St. Joseph Catholic Church
Ashtabula, Ohio

Tom, John, Jon, Emily, Bill, Kat

Jon, Kat, Bill, Tom, John & Emily

John's 75th Birthday, at the home of Jon C. Ricker
in Mentor, Ohio, May 30, 2011

Other Titles from Trillium Press
Available on Amazon.com

Something Familiar
Poems and Short Stories
by Kat Ricker
ISBN 1-590281-52-7
$10.00

This collection embraces storytelling about characters you'll recognize, from life in smalltown America, the farm, to the strange conversations of otherworldly matters heard on the metro bus, and even a fairy or two. Plus, this book features a photo of John C. Ricker right on the cover!

The Daculi Witch Chronicles
by Kat Ricker
Edited by John C. Ricker
ISBN 978-0-615-34669-4
$19.95

The Daculi Witch Chronicles weaves history with fiction to present the story of a line of women struggling to live their lives during the Great European Witch Hunts. This adventure flows through major moments in history, tying them together to chronicle an extraordinary family line and reinvestigate witchcraft from a fresh perspective.

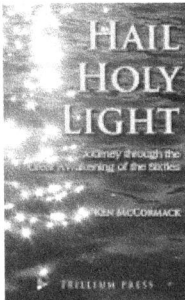

Hail, Holy Light: A Journey Through
the Great Awakening of the Sixties
by Ken McCormack
ISBN-13: 978-0615529332
ISBN-10: 061552933X
$12.00

An in-depth historical and philosophical examination of the era of two cultural icons, John F. Kennedy and Aldous Huxley, followed by an inspiring memoir of the spiritual transformation of the author coming out of the consciousness awakening of the Sixties.

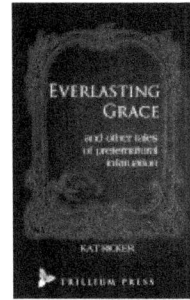

Everlasting Grace
and other stories of
preternatural infatuation
by Kat Ricker
Edited by Rebecca Dobrinski
ISBN 978-0-615-96811-7
$9.95

Tales of the fervent and frequently forlorn devotion between mortals and beings from different realms—vampires, elementals, spectres. Ungovernable attractions press the veil of reality and defy the cautions of reason.

Other Titles from Trillium Press
Available on Amazon.com